THIS
WE'LL
DEFEND

THIS
WE'LL
DEFEND

A NONCOMBAT
VETERAN ON
WAR AND ITS
AFTERMATH

PAUL CRENSHAW

THE UNIVERSITY OF NORTH CAROLINA PRESS *Chapel Hill*

Designed by Jamison Cockerham
Set in Scala and Logbond
by codeMantra, Inc.

Manufactured in the United States of America

The University of North Carolina Press has been a
member of the Green Press Initiative since 2003.

Cover photograph © iStockphoto.com/brunorbs

LIBRARY OF CONGRESS CATALOGING-IN-PUBLICATION DATA
Names: Crenshaw, Paul, 1972– author.
Title: This we'll defend : a noncombat veteran on
    war and its aftermath / Paul Crenshaw.
Description: Chapel Hill : The University of North Carolina
    Press, [2019] | Includes bibliographical references.
Identifiers: LCCN 2018052924| ISBN 9781469651071
    (pbk : alk. paper) | ISBN 9781469651088 (ebook)
Subjects: LCSH: War—Psychological aspects. | Soldiers—
    United States. | Veterans—United States.
Classification: LCC U22.3 .C74 2019 | DDC 355.0092 [B] —dc23
    LC record available at https://lccn.loc.gov/2018052924

These essays originally appeared in the following publications, for
which grateful acknowledgement is given: "Names," *Hobart*; "Lying,"
Connecticut Review; "The Size of Their Toys," *Word Riot*; "Drill
Sergeant, Yes, Drill Sergeant," *Memoir*; "Cadence," *Hotel Amerika*; "Is
There Anyone Downrange?," *Pinball*; "Flight," *Eclectica*; "Movement,"
Diagram; "On Fire," *North American Review*; "Feldgrau," *Pithead Chapel*;
"Essay in Five Photographs," *Tampa Review*; "The Hornet among
Us," "When the War Began," *War, Literature and the Arts*; "This Is My
Rifle," *As It Ought to Be*; "Red Dawn," *The Rumpus*; "Shock and Awe,"
Brevity; "My New War Essay," *Seneca Review*; "What Happens Next,"
Oxford American. "Names" also appeared in *Best American Essays 2016*;
"Cadence" also appeared in *Best American Essays 2018*; "The Hornet
among Us" also appeared in *The Pushcart Prize Anthology 2017*.

CONTENTS

THIS
WE'LL
DEFEND

NAMES

Keller was Killer and Weaver was Weiner and Penn was Penis or just a dick. Benavidez was Bean Burrito and Ellenberger was Hamburger and Alarid got called asshole more than his real name. Hoteling was Hot Ding-a-ling. Ramirez was Rape-kit. I was Crankshaft or Cumshot or Cocksucker, depending on who was doing the calling, whether my fellow soldiers or the drill sergeants who stalked the halls of Basic Training scowling behind mirrored shades, their boot steps ricocheting like rifles.

Crawford got called Crotchface. Rhea became Gonorrhea after Talley(whacker) scrawled the "gonor" in front of "Rhea," though with a name like Rhea it was only a matter of time before someone put the "gonor" in front. Clapp was too easy and so no one even bothered changing his name, only put "the" in front of "Clapp," and Syphers couldn't escape Syphilis any more than any of us could escape Fort Sill, where we found ourselves in the summer of 1990. Sackett was Sackbreath and Swallows got asked what he swallowed more times than I care to count, though we all laughed every time, exhausted as we were from long hours and little sleep and hard training, our eyes red and bones tired and some fear lingering deep inside that made us think such jokes were funny.

Nguyen we just called Gook. Ten Bears became Ten Bears Fucking. Black we called White and White we called Black and

1

Green we called Baby Shit and Brown was just Shit. Bevilacqua was Aqua Velva, which was getting off pretty light as far as names went so sometimes we called him Bologna or Ballsack.

Leaks had a leaky dick, and Lebowitz was a lesbian, to which he would proclaim loudly that he was, indeed, a lesbian, trapped in a man's body, another lame joke that we all laughed at because there was nothing else to do, no other way to get through the long days than to laugh and name each other dicks and diseases and dysfunctions. At eighteen, we were barely grown boys wielding weapons of war while bombs went off in our little part of the world and the ground shook beneath us. Our drill sergeants were constantly calling us cocks and cunts, threatening us with physical violence. We were scared all the time—of our drill sergeants, of the base where we had been sent to train, of the future—and to keep the fear from flying out we flung bravado at one another in our choice of words. We were all dysfunctional, we thought, for we were told so by the drill sergeants all the time, from the first long days when we arrived at Fort Sill and cried sometimes in this harsh new place, through the hot afternoons of drill and ceremony, marching in big round wheels under the summer sun, all the called commands a way to discipline us, make us move as one unit instead of fifty different men, like the naming was to break us down so we could pull closer together; through Basic Rifle Marksmanship and the hand grenade course and the bayonet course, where we stabbed dummies of Russian soldiers; through med training, where we learned to treat sucking chest wounds and splint broken limbs and administer antidotes for anthrax and sarin and mustard gas; through morning eight-mile runs and evening mail call; and even through the too-short nights. We could shoot and stab and knock out hundreds of push-ups but were constantly derided, a strategy meant to demean us but also demand that we rise above such degradation.

I'll say we did. A man can get used to being called dickhead or dumbfuck or some other designation, to being named by his nationality or upbringing, some physical attribute like Aaronson's Dicknose or Biobaku's almost blue skin. Twenty-five years later I laugh at being called Crankshaft and Cumshot. Benavidez's big belly did seem to hold a lot of burritos, and when we graduated and were waiting to be released for the last time, some of us to go to college and some of us to war, we shook hands hard. "I'll miss you, motherfucker," we said, and other words that only made sense in light of living with fifty men for months, hearing farts and of football and girls they'd fucked, all the things men say to make themselves sound stronger.

Perhaps we were scared of letting one another know how we felt so we hid everything behind a screen. Perhaps all our words are only screens for what we might say if we were better people, or perhaps we only use words that fit what world we find ourselves in. Our voices were hoarse from yelling all the time, making us sound much older than we were, and we had to shave every morning now, look at ourselves in the mirror and see the men we might become.

In our final days of training, as we wound down toward release and finally began to relax a little, Saddam Hussein invaded Kuwait and we were all called together so the drill sergeants could tell us we were going to war. We stood there in stunned silence until someone—Talleywhacker, maybe, or Hot Ding-a-ling—said we'd fuck that fucking towel-headed sand nigger right in the fucking asshole is what we would do, and we all cheered with our hoarse voices standing there in our young boots.

But later that night after lights-out, as we lay in our bunks in the darkness, we had no words to contain how we felt. The silence stood around us like stones. We could hear bombs off in the distant part of the base, as if the war had already come. The windows rattled softly in their panes. There were no jokes, no called names. Only a hundred quiet conversations, Alarid or Benavidez or Talley whispering across the big bay dorm, "Hey Crenshaw, hey man, are you scared?"

LYING

A few months after the Gulf War ended, I found myself telling people I tried to go. I was in the National Guard then, and though my unit was never activated during the war, I fabricated the idea that I had tried to enlist full-time so I could fight. This was a lie I told whenever the conversation rolled around to war, or the military, or dying or honor or death, but after the third or fourth time I said it I started to believe it.

I never entertained the notion seriously. Like most of us, I watched the war from home. Many nights in college, my roommate and I sat before the TV, sipping whiskey and watching bombs fall on Baghdad. Late at night, after a fifth of Jack Daniels, we would squint one-eyed at the green glow on the screen, and even later, with dawn creeping through the windows and cigarette butts smoldering in the ashtrays and the first stirrings deep in the bowels of the dorms beginning, we would raise our glasses and lie to each other about how much we wished we were there.

When we woke late in the afternoon, we'd walk through the cold sunless day to the cafeteria and eat silently, watching the world go on around us. We went back to the dorm in time to catch the six o'clock news, to see the grim face of Dan Rather describe the deaths that day, the number of sorties flown over Iraq, the number of troops continuing to mass in the desert. On our bulletin board we had a collage of newspaper clippings, mostly photos of Apache helicopters and A-10 Thunderbolts. We stole *Time* and *Newsweek* from the library and *USA Today* from a guy down the hall who had it delivered each morning. Each night, after the evening news had gone off and the endless sitcoms had started, we drove back to the liquor store and then returned to our small room and watched the world at war.

By the time the ground war started and the Iraqi Army began surrendering in the tens of thousands, the country had been reduced to rubble. When CNN rolled in with the troops, the desert had become a wasteland. Iraqi tanks and trucks were forgotten along the sides of the roads, cars abandoned as people tried to flee, the broken highways littered with the detritus of their exodus: chairs and tables and dolls and deflated soccer balls. Battleships in the Red Sea hammered the coast. Bombers protected by fighters carpet-bombed the Republican Guard. The navy and marines feinted an amphibious landing to show that we could fight by sea or land or air. Shattered buildings in central Baghdad proclaimed our inerrant missiles while oil fires burned in the desert night under a sky where the star of Bethlehem had once shone.

One weekend a month, my roommate and I drove to our hometown for our National Guard drills. We spit shined our boots and shaved and dressed in our uniforms and entered the armory for morning formation. Inside the armory, the ceiling vaulted overhead. The floor was concrete, and the first sergeant's voice echoed and clanged from the walls and ceiling as he called roll in the morning. Most of the time we could not understand what he was saying. He might have been telling us we were going to war.

After morning formation, my friends and I disappeared. We'd hide out in the backs of Humvees or else spend half the day in the latrine, hoping no one came in. Our hometown was not far from a military base, and sometimes we'd hear planes streaking past like the distant threat of war, though we'd always tuck ourselves deeper into our hiding spot and try harder to sleep. Some mornings we loaded up after first formation and headed to the fields. Here we played at war, putting up tents in the cold and listening to the rattle of artillery in the distance, though most of the time we hid after the tents had been erected. If someone found us—the first sergeant or the captain—we would be put to work, and so we hid as much as possible, waiting for the weekend to be over so we could go back to college and skip classes.

This is my memory of war: drunk nights before the TV, then sleeping all day to wake and drive to the liquor store to do it all again. Sleeping during our weekend guard drills or hiding somewhere listening to the phantom sound of fighters overhead. Nowhere in it is the idea of entering the war. I'm not sure now how I would have even gone about it. I suppose I could have talked to an army recruiter or my captain, but none of those things ever happened. Like most of war, my memories of it are lies.

— — — — — — — — — — —

We have always played at war. As children, my brother and I would dress up in my father's military fatigues. We'd slip his too-big combat boots on and flop his BDU caps over our faces and salute each other as general or corporal or sergeant. We broke into his gear and followed each other around the house at night with his flashlights. We stole his entrenching tool and dug holes in which to bury the bodies of the enemies we had killed. High in his closet, guns gleamed at us, and though we were forbidden to touch them at any time, we returned often when he was away to imagine the force and power they held. At my grandfather's house, we rifled through the closets until we found his World War II uniform. We dug through old photos of him at some military base, a place that exists now only in the distance of time.

Out of doors we played cowboys and Indians, G.I. Joe, *Star Wars*. We recreated epic battles, acting out scenes from movies. With other kids that lived within walking distance, we separated into groups, blasting fake guns at each other. We argued over whether our opponent had been hit and whether he should be dead. In video games, we saved the world from missiles and space invaders, then fought each other with tanks and airplanes.

As we grew older our games progressed in intensity and violence. Behind the house where I grew up, I'm sure there are still small piles of hardened plastic from the toy soldiers my brother and I melted and small graveyards of birds buried in the woods from snowy days when my best friend and I grew bored and wanted to kill. We hunted constantly, stalking the woods with, first, toy bows and arrows, then BB guns, then .410s and .22s. When we could not find any game to kill, we would just blast away at whatever was handy: birds, bottles, abandoned barns way out in the woods.

On trips to the nearest city, we drove through Fort Chaffee, along roads lined with steel fences topped by razor wire, over roads pitted and patched from errant artillery. Behind the steel fences, mounds of earth rose like old tribal burial grounds. Beneath them large caches of ammunition were stored, the fence along those areas marked with violent orange signs warning away anyone without the proper authorization. Planes overhead broke the sound barrier, and the constant rain of artillery sounded like thunder rumbling in the distance.

In high school we read *Hamlet* and *Macbeth* and *Julius Caesar*. We read *Alas, Babylon*, a novel in which the world destroys and then tries to rebuild itself. We read "An Occurrence at Owl Creek Bridge" and "Chickamauga" by Ambrose Bierce and *For Whom the Bell Tolls* by Ernest Hemingway. We read *The Iliad* and *The Odyssey* and *Lord of the Flies*. We read *All Quiet on the Western Front* and *Across Five Aprils*, *The Red Badge of Courage* and *Catch-22*, *The Scarlet Pimpernel* and *The Sun Also Rises*, as if war were the only human emotion worth writing about.

——— —— —— —— —— —— —— —— —— —— ——

I enlisted in the National Guard at the start of my senior year of high school. This was 1989, and all the wars were over. The Berlin Wall had fallen. The Cold War was ending. Shortly after I enlisted I wore my uniform to school one day. This was my army recruiter's idea—that by wearing my uniform I would advertise for the army and, he thought, convince my friends to join, which would make more money for the recruiter. My friends saluted me in the hall. They called me Sergeant Slaughter or G.I. Joe. One teacher—a man of a different generation— called me Beetle Bailey and, when I failed to answer a question correctly, Gomer Pyle.

My junior year I had taken the ASVAB, the prerequisite test for military service. Over a hundred of us—all male, all juniors and seniors in high school, all with only vague notions of both the military and our futures—gathered in the school's cafeteria. It was noisy and crowded. Paper airplanes winged overhead. A marine lance corporal with a balding head passed out the exams. He wore glasses and looked nothing like the marines we saw on commercials.

A few weeks later, the phone calls from recruiters began. I had scored high enough on the test to make myself a target, and they called ceaselessly, asking each night how I planned on paying for college, had I ever thought of the military as a career, did I want to serve my country. My grandfather had served twenty-six years in the National Guard, a career that spanned from World War II to the Vietnam era, when he retired as a colonel. Both he and my father extolled the virtues of military service, citing good pay and health insurance, a chance for a career.

Not long after that, I found myself on a bus to Little Rock, Arkansas, to be poked and prodded and inspected and finally, once all the test results were back in and I was considered fit for military service, to raise my right hand and swear allegiance to the United States and the state of Arkansas. Not long after that, I was on a plane to Fort Sill, Oklahoma, and not long after that, I woke one morning, just a few weeks before I graduated from Basic Training, to learn that Saddam Hussein had invaded Kuwait and that soon another war would begin, and sometime after that, I found myself telling people I had tried to get myself shipped to the Middle East in order to fight.

— — — — — — — — — — —

In *The Things They Carried*, Tim O'Brien writes, "In any war story, but especially a true one, it's difficult to separate what happened from what seemed to happen." This is not a war story. It's not even an "almost war story." But here are some things that did happen:

On the Fourth of July in 1990, my fellow soldiers and I sat on a small hill at Fort Sill, Oklahoma, and clasped our arms around each other and sang "God Bless the USA" along with Lee Greenwood, who had been flown in to perform that day. In the distance, cannons fired a fifty-gun salute to America, each shot rattling to the far hills. Later, we got drunk on beer we were commanded not to drink and told stories about how often we would get laid when we got home. Fireworks unfurled overhead, each cluster its own star, and it seemed then that where we were was a good place to be.

One year later, after the war had ended and the troops were returning home, my friends and I, at Advanced Individual Training at Fort Jackson, South Carolina, were mistaken for soldiers returning home from Desert Storm. We were thanked and hugged and had our hands shaken by men and women and children, until finally a radio reporter interviewed us, asking how it felt to return home after defending freedom. One by one we looked at her, then at each other, and after some time we told her that it felt just fine indeed, that we were grateful to be home and grateful for all the support we had received from friends and strangers alike.

Every summer in the National Guard we spent two weeks playing war. We showed up early Saturday morning and loaded all our vehicles and equipment and drove thirty miles in convoy to Fort Chaffee. Already the bombs would be falling in the distance as other National Guard units fired artillery rounds or Air Guard units dropped payload, and sometimes at night, waking disoriented on a small cot somewhere in the breathless tent, it was hard to understand where we were, how we had gotten there.

And in the summer of 1995, on the fifth anniversary of the invasion of Kuwait, I left the military forever. No one gave any speeches. I had gone to weekend drill the month before. That August, I did not. For years I would dream I was still in the military, that I was late for formation, or that my unit had been activated and I had been recalled because a new war had cropped up somewhere in the world. By that time, I was married, with a daughter on the way, and I would wake not quite breathing heavily, not quite afraid that the dream might come true.

Here are some things that seemed to happen:

It seems we watched the war every night in college, sitting on the edges of our beds, seeing the missiles fly. It seems a sort of fear and paranoia and exhilaration got inside us each time the sky lit up, so that sometimes we cheered fiercely before falling silent once again. Night after night after night, it seems, until the war crept inside us and shadowed our waking hours so that we skipped classes or ghost walked to them and sat not listening, instead seeing the green glow of night vision traced into our minds. Now I suspect this is not true but only what it seems in memory. In all likelihood, there were only three or four nights at the beginning of the war in which we watched. After that, I'm sure, our nights monitoring the bombs and flashes lessened to hours and then to minutes, until finally we would simply glance at the screen once a day, then change the channel and watch reruns of *G.I. Joe*.

It also seems we are unaffected by the wars we fight. My father narrowly avoided Vietnam. He joined the National Guard to keep from being drafted. Years later, he would advise me to join for the college money and life insurance, and when Desert Storm began, he assured me that my unit would not be activated. My grandfather often smiled when he told stories of World War II and Korea. He never talked of battle and death but rather of hunting pheasant on weekend passes in Korea or of the cities he had seen in Europe. My stepfather was the same way—his stories of Desert Storm consist of the Arab culture he saw, the way the desert stretches out unbroken before you, the way the sand gets in your eyes and ears and nose and mouth. He speaks of the uncomfortable days, the poor diet, the constant boredom. He speaks of missing home. Rarely will he speak of artillery rounds mushrooming upward all around or bodies riddled with bullets on the side of the road. It seems perhaps having seen them once is enough.

And it seems I tried to fight in Desert Storm. I'm sure I told people this. I'm equally sure it never happened. At some point I might have considered enlisting in the army full-time. But I'm not sure when. It might have been when I was seventeen, long before the war began, when I was considering what path my life might take. It might have been long after the war was over and I was looking for a career after flunking out of college. More likely, if it occurred at all, it was somewhere between what happened and what seemed to happen.

— — — — — — — — — — —

I was raised to never lie, that liars are not to be trusted, and that a man who will lie will also cheat and steal—and is, in fact, not a man at all. This lie sticks with me. As far as I know it did not hurt anyone. It is not the outcome but the fabrication itself, the reasoning behind it. I suppose I was trying to impress people, a fact I'm not proud of but something I must face in any attempt to find truth. I suppose I could have said that I had seen war and death all around me, that I had killed a man, and given some line about how you don't know how valuable life is until you have taken one, but at least I was not that pretentious.

Still, it forces me now to examine the why. It's a story I told not to entertain or enlighten or educate those who heard it, which any good story should do, but to fill in a part of me, a part of all of us, that has always existed. I wanted to align myself with men who aim guns toward other men with guns, men who face death in defense of an idea, whatever that idea may be. In our conflicted psyches we value war, and I wanted to be valued, to be tested and found passing. It is not a good answer but the only one I can find. A fitting end, then, to this story.

And the beginning of another, perhaps one that will educate or enlighten:

Years after he returned home from the Korean War, my grandfather applied for a job at a biological agent manufacturing plant. I have never seen the place, but in my mind I always imagine a paper mill, with its requisite stink and ash and soot, but the reality is most likely much less severe, and the second image that comes to mind is of white-coated technicians with surgical masks covering their faces and radial dials testing the air.

My grandfather was called in for an interview. I always think he was still limping from the wound he took in Korea, though this was in the early 60s. The plant had been constructed not long before, as the Cold War constructed itself out of the ruins of World War II. I try to imagine my grandfather walking the long halls of the plant. I imagine him looking into labs where techs fill vials and create serums, Bunsen burners singeing the stale air.

That is my imagination, though. What really happened was my grandfather sat in an office speaking with a man whose name has been lost. According to my grandfather, they did not speak about the job for which he was applying. Instead, they talked about their children. They swapped stories of World War II and Korea, both of them having been there. Outside the walls of the office, men were breeding toxins to spill out into the air we breathe, but inside, they spoke of the weather and what was happening in Southeast Asia. In the decade before, TV screens had begun beaming images into our houses, into our hearts and heads, and war had become cold, creeping into everything we knew and had known, becoming a presence inside all of us.

After some time, my grandfather asked about the job, wondering when the interview would begin. The man, my grandfather tells me, spread his hands to encompass the entire plant.

"This is the interview," he said. He picked up his pen and clicked it rapidly. "We just needed to see how you would react to being in the building. Some people think the nerve agents we make can get inside them, that just by being here they will become infected."

I don't know what my grandfather's response was. But I know that after a while he left the office and never returned. I can only speculate as to why. I think he began wondering what airborne viruses might even then be creeping inside him that might eventually be passed down to his children and his children's children, so he left and never returned. But I also think that it was too late—that the agents of war were already swimming through my bloodstream, years before I was born.

THE SIZE OF
THEIR TOYS

If I could warp drive or time travel or beam myself to anywhere or anywhen, I would go to the floor of my bedroom, circa 1978, where I sometimes spent the whole day lining up my little green army men opposite one another and forcing them to fight. I bought a bag of 144 soldiers every few weeks because things kept happening to them—they got run over by the lawn mower or sucked up in the vacuum cleaner or "accidentally" tossed down the old well outside our house—and when I got a new bag I'd open it carefully, inhaling plastic and paint, then take out the soldiers one by one, sorting them into squads, all the kneeling bazookas together, all the prone riflemen side by side. There were mine detectors and radio operators and a few officers with pistols. There were flame throwers and mortar launchers and machine gunners, and I set them all up every Saturday morning before the good cartoons came on—Bugs Bunny fighting Elmer Fudd or Daffy Duck or Yosemite Sam over gold or swords or whether it was duck or wabbit season—and aimed their weapons at one another.

Some days, to make the war more realistic, I would steal a bottle of my mother's red fingernail polish and paint blood on the soldiers. I'd take my pocketknife and carve away pieces of their shoulders or faces, then wrap their wounds with gauze. I had a die-cast Chinook helicopter and an F-4 Phantom with a mouth and jaws painted near the front, and the F-4 ran cover missions over the prone soldiers while the Chinook began airlifting them away. When my brother came in the room and stomped around yelling "nuke" until all my careful lines were scattered and all my soldiers had bent rifles or broken bazookas, I wished I had airlifted them away sooner and hid them from his mass destruction.

Or perhaps in my time travel I would go to the toy aisle at Wal-Mart after the new *Stars Wars* action figures have come out and are hanging in their plastic cases with scenes from the movie on the cardboard backs, their lightsabers or blaster pistols at their sides. Next to Han and Luke and Leia are bags and bags of army men, and next to those are disc guns and potato guns and cap guns. Next to the guns are plastic hand grenades and self-propelled rocket launchers and cap bombs shaped like real bombs. Farther down the aisle are the View-Masters and Simons, the Magic Markers and Crayola crayons, the Etch A Sketches and Lite-Brites and See 'n Says, but I'm drawn to action figures and Rock 'Em Sock 'Em Robots, to water pistols and Red Ryder BB guns. I'm drawn to the dark side of the force.

Or I would go to my living room in the early 80s, when my parents bought me an Atari 2600 for Christmas and my family gathered to play *Asteroids* and *Missile Command* and *Space Invaders* and *Combat*, the cartridge that came with the system, a simple game in which you and your opponent fired ricocheting bullets at each other from tanks or airplanes or helicopters. *Asteroids* placed you in a tiny ship in the middle of giant hunks of rock caroming around. There was no plot, no story line, only more and more rocks hurtling at you from the depths of space, which was also where the aliens came from in *Space Invaders*, their antennae waving as they marched down the black sky toward Earth. *Missile Command* asked you to save the world from falling missiles, and when the missiles struck, as they always did, eventually, a mushroom cloud rose over the cities of the world and the screen turned a sickly shade of yellow before fading to black.

I used to own a starfighter from *Buck Rogers* and a little Twiki figurine that made noises and lit up. I had a Snoopy alarm clock with a loud, obnoxious bell ring that I hated, but I loved Snoopy because he fought the Red Baron from atop his doghouse. When I got bored in school, I drew pictures of the Cylons from *Battlestar Galactica*, the Colonial Vipers and Raiders. On rainy days we played Monopoly, where we tried to take over the bank, and Risk, where we tried to take over the world. In an act of maliciousness that I sometimes still despise him for, my brother burned all my little green army men with a can of hairspray and a lighter, melting their plastic faces into pools of plastic goo, and once, after a fight, when he felt the way only brothers can feel toward one another, he burned my *Star Wars* figures, and I certainly still despise him for that, not only because some of them would be worth a lot of money, but there's a feeling inside me, foolish though it may be, that if I could find some of the toys I used to own as a child, I might remember what it was like to be one.

— — — — — — — — — — — —

I kept all my toys in a giant football chest that eventually cracked and split open. But for a long time, it sat in my closet beneath a blue blazer I wore only to church, where I would sneak one of my *Star Wars* figures—usually Vader or a stormtrooper—and walk him up and down the back of the pew in front of me until my grandmother made me quit, and then I would enact quiet battles on my thigh or on top of the Bible in my lap.

Besides Vader and a handful of stormtroopers in various dress—TIE fighter stormtroopers in black flight suits and Endor moon bike-riding stormtroopers and machine gunner stormtroopers that came with machine gun and tripod—I had Luke and Leia and Obi-Wan, Han and Chewie and C-3PO and R2-D2 and Boba Fett and IG-88 and the lizard bounty hunter whose name escapes me now. I had rebel soldiers with their German Wehrmacht–like helmets and X-wing fighters and B-wing fighters and a cast-iron Millennium Falcon about the size my palm is now. It had a plastic gray satellite dish on top that swiveled 360 degrees, and through the Plexiglas windows you could see tiny little men sitting at the controls as they veered around the universe of my bedroom. I had a foot-tall stormtrooper and a Chewbacca complete with a crossbow laser that was the absolute coolest thing in the world at age eight, with perhaps the exception of lightsabers, which Darth Vader and Luke and Obi-Wan carried. Boba Fett wore a big missile on his back and wielded a laser rifle. Luke Skywalker came in X-wing Luke and Bespin Luke and Jedi Luke. Han Solo had his space jockey outfit and his Hoth outfit, and *Return of the Jedi* Leia wore a chain bra and a real chain around her neck (another model from the same movie wore her Endor moon outfit, but of course boys were drawn to the chain bra version).

I wanted them all. I wanted the action figures, and I wanted a lightsaber and crossbow and a machine gun and Boba Fett armor. I wanted to pilot the Millennium Falcon, or a TIE fighter, or a Colonial Viper. I wanted to sit near Spock on the bridge of the USS *Enterprise* as Captain Kirk called for Warp 4, as Scotty and McCoy beamed down with one of the red-shirted guys you knew wasn't going to make it back. My brother and I made that little whooshing sound the automatic doors on the *Enterprise* made whenever we entered the house or went into the kitchen, where our *Star Wars* commemorative glasses were stacked in the cabinets beside our *Empire Strikes Back* lunch boxes.

I had Spock and Kirk figures too, Kirk in the yellow captain's shirt and Spock in blue, and a model *Enterprise* I put together one rainy afternoon while my parents yelled at each other in the living room. For a long time, I wanted to be one of the Hawkmen from the *Flash Gordon* movie, which came out in 1980, about the time my parents' marriage was disintegrating. After school, I came home to an empty house, but *Star Trek* came on at four, Kirk and Spock and McCoy sailing through the universe and righting wrongs, always hoping the next leap will be the leap home, but no, that's the theme from *Quantum Leap*, which didn't appear until 1989, about the time I was trying to decide between college and the military, or perhaps suicide if neither of those things worked out.

There is a temptation, even now, to scroll through the vintage toys on eBay, the Millennium Falcons and X-wing fighters, the Godzillas, the foot-tall stormtroopers. The Obi-Wans and differently clothed Leias, the Greedos and Hammerheads, the Lego Star Destroyer that sells for close to $2,000 on Amazon.

The temptation, of course, is to return. This is why vintage *Star Wars* figures sell for so much—men my age trying to recapture their youth. This is why, as we grow older, we tend to accumulate more and more, as if by surrounding ourselves with symbols we might surround ourselves with substance, make some sense of where the years have flown, of whether time has somehow warped or we have beamed ourselves into adult bodies.

Sometime in my childhood, Reagan came up with a plan to put missiles and lasers in space in case the Soviet Union ever launched its ICBMs, and sometime in the late 80s I traded my toys for guns, first hunting rifles and then an M16. In 1991, the first Gulf War appeared on our TV screens like magic or special effects, something out of a movie or our childhood imaginations. Not long ago, I received a catalog in the mail from which I could order Glocks and Desert Eagles and Remington Model 870 Express HD twelve-gauge pump-action shotguns, complete with riot grip and tactical rail and fifty-round bandoleer. I could order box upon box of cartridges and shells, from surplus Russian and Hungarian calibers to 5.56 NATO rounds, and I could order laser sights and conversion kits and carbon-fiber handguards, all of which sound a little like science fiction, but there is no fiction here.

I wonder if our fear of Soviet missiles drew our attentions toward the stars and made us think of alien invaders, or if we've always feared what might fall on us out of the sky or arrive from the dark of space. It occurs to me now that we never had a chance to win those old Atari games because there was no way to win. They always, always, ended in death and destruction. The waves of asteroids or invading enemies came faster and faster until they destroyed the world, but at Christmas, cold outside, snow and ice on the roads, we simply took turns trying to save it, laughing when we failed, secure in our knowledge we could always restart and try again.

Had I been born in 1997 or 2000, as my daughters were, I would wish for wands from *Harry Potter*, Katniss's bow, the immortality of Team Edward or Team Jacob, themes programmed into them by movies and TV shows and advertisements as they are taught from a young age to buy and buy and buy, targeted as if by heat-seeking missiles or photon torpedoes. On all our favorite shows and games, missiles fell from the sky and spaceships destroyed entire planets in a never-ending thirst for conquest, but I didn't care about that because of the way the Millennium Falcon fit into the curve of my palm, its die-cast weight so heavy, so substantial. As if I, too, could fly, could warp drive myself wherever and whenever I wanted, see all the corners of the far universe.

I always go back to the toy aisle at Wal-Mart or the living room one lost Christmas, with wrapping paper strewn across the floor and just-opened shiny toys lying all around. Or my bedroom floor early in the morning, before my parents divorced. Before acne and awkwardness. Before college and a family and the subtle yet sudden realization I have grown older. Before any awareness of wars in the world, only those on the screen or those you created, wars you knew would turn out all right. Back before the sky filled with missiles and drones like something straight out of science fiction, before the realization the world could actually end. Back to when the top of the toy chest comes off, it's raining outside, and the only difficult choice you have to make is which toy to play with, which world to explore, which war to bring to a victorious end.

DRILL SERGEANT,
YES,
DRILL SERGEANT

A few days before I shipped to Basic Training, I watched *Full Metal Jacket* with several friends who were also shipping out soon. In the movie, Matthew Modine is a wisecracking marine, and R. Lee Ermey is a volatile drill sergeant fond of vulgar language, with a propensity to smack recruits upside the head, and halfway through the movie Vincent D'Onofrio's character blows his own head off right after he shoots R. Lee Ermey in the chest in the bathroom late the night before he was supposed to ship to Vietnam. Being eighteen, my friends and I completely missed the subtext as well as the subsequent scenes of death and destruction in Vietnam, and for three days we stalked around like R. Lee Ermey telling Vincent D'Onofrio's character that he is a slimy fucking walrus-looking piece of shit and other lines from the movie.

My time in the army opens with a long trip to Fort Sill, Oklahoma. From the windows of a military bus, the base looks like those fake towns the government built in the Southwest desert before detonating the atomic bomb. We arrive late in the night, passing the pawn shops and board-windowed bars of the city of Lawton, through the stone gates and the chain link fences, and down the empty streets of Fort Sill. Long rows of barracks stretch out before us. The streets are deserted but for MPs in a military jeep. At the time, I assume they are looking for trespassers or terrorists but later learn that since Fort Sill is a training fort, they spend a lot of time searching for men who have gone AWOL.

A placid drill sergeant meets us when we get off the bus. His quiet demeanor is disappointing, despite the fact that he is well over six feet tall, with arms thick as my legs, and he wears sunglasses that blank out his eyes even though it is three in the morning. We form in a ragged line before him, thirty boys fresh out of high school, while he explains that this is Reception Station, where we will be in-processed before being shipped to a different part of the fort for Basic Training. He stands looking at us for a long time, hands clasped behind his back, then turns abruptly on one heel.

"Follow me," he says.

From the back, one kid even skinnier than the rest of us says, "Yes, sir."

The drill sergeant stops, head half-turned over his shoulder. I think he must have been drugged or perhaps beaten into submission—he is nothing like R. Lee Ermey. I'd been expecting a drill sergeant who would yell and scream, slap someone upside the head, or put a fist in their gut, a man so dedicated to his beloved army that he would take any steps necessary to mold new recruits into soldiers. We would all hate him at first but after a while would come to respect and admire him for the way he motivated us to be better soldiers and, ultimately, human beings.

"I work for a living," he tells us. "Don't call me 'sir.'"

"Yes, sir."

He has turned to go and now stops again. He draws a deep breath. I think a torrent is coming, a screaming tantrum where he tells us what pieces of shit we are, how we have no right to be in the army and we'd be better off if we took a long walk off a short pier. Instead he lets out his breath.

"You answer, 'Drill Sergeant, yes, Drill Sergeant.' That understood?"

"Drill Sergeant, yes, Drill Sergeant," we all say.

He nods once and leads us toward our barracks. I start to think, "Maybe this won't be so bad," then correct myself: "Drill Sergeant, maybe this won't be so bad, Drill Sergeant."

The barracks smell of feet and old farts. The mattresses are cum stained from years of masturbation. We are issued a sheet and a wool blanket, though by this time we are all so tired we simply fall on the cum stains and sleep in our clothes. I'd caught a bus the morning before and rode two hours to Little Rock, where I caught a short flight to Dallas. After a five-hour layover at DFW, I caught an even shorter flight to Lawton, where another bus picked me up. It had taken me close to ten hours to reach Fort Sill, which was a four-hour drive from my house.

We are not woken by a shouting drill sergeant or a bugle playing reveille, no R. Lee Ermey shouting "Drop your cocks and grab your socks." The same drill sergeant from the night before enters quietly, flips on the light, and asks, in what seems a very polite voice, for us to wake up. In the gray daylight creeping through the windows, the barracks are old and crumbling. We sit up, rubbing our eyes, red and tired from lack of sleep.

He tells us the first order of business is getting the barracks squared away and proceeds to show us how to make our bunks. His name is Green, and despite the lateness of the hour he went to bed, he doesn't seem tired. He shows us how to place the sheet, how to fold the blanket into tight hospital corners. When he finishes, he stands back and admires his work. I am a little disappointed he doesn't bounce a quarter off of it.

"Now you," he says.

I am just finishing my bunk when I feel him looming over me. I stand back to let him see. He shakes his head slowly and sadly, as if I have dashed all his hopes and dreams for America with my poor performance at bed making.

"That looks like D-O-D-O," he says. He lowers his sunglasses so he can look over them at me. "You know what that spells?"

"Dodo?" I say, like the extinct bird.

"Doo-doo, son. Caca. Poop. Shit."

He reaches down and rips the sheet and blanket off, then stands watching while I remake it. I attack the corners, stretching the wool blanket tight. I have learned my first military word: doo-doo, a metaphor that simply means something, as in a job you have completed, that looks like shit.

— — — — — — — — — — —

Smith, R.—so designated to distinguish him from Smith, S.—has a father and three older brothers in the military and considers the week in Reception Station his chance to show all of us how much he knows about the military. He tells us that this isn't shit, that after Reception Station we will be sent to the shit, where "the motherfucking drills will be all up in our heavy shit like flies on shit."

After we have the barracks squared away, we stand outside in formation. Smith, R., tells us some heavy shit is coming down. It is hot, close to ninety at five in the morning. Drill Sergeant Green is explaining the position of attention: arms at your sides, thumb and forefinger resting along the seams of your trousers, feet at a forty-five-degree angle with the heels touching.

"Do not lock your knees," Drill Sergeant Green says. "Locking your knees will cause you to faint."

Immediately three men pretend to faint, staggering to the ground in the hope they will be allowed to sleep longer. Drill Sergeant Green smiles: he has been expecting this. He takes smelling salts from his shirt pocket and chases one of the men around. The other two decide that they did not really faint, and it occurs to me that this is a place where we have to learn a new way to stand, and that if we do not learn correctly there will be consequences.

While we are standing in formation, several of the new recruits are detailed for KP. At this point I do not know what "detail" or "KP" mean, and since Smith, R., is one of the ones detailed for KP, I do not find out, but it is a bit quieter without the observations of Smith, R., that "most of you punk-ass bitches will be crying for your momma's titties the first time your fucking drill gets all up in your shit."

After the detail team has left, we are issued clothing. We stand in line outside an old crumbling building while the heat builds. We are still wearing our civilian clothes, and a company of marines point us out as they jog by. They have high-and-tight haircuts, and they are dressed in BDUs, boots slicked sharp, hats pulled low. They have muscles and slim, military mustaches, and they look like they have been through some heavy shit. We all stand a bit straighter as they jog by, trying to look tough.

Inside, we sidle slowly down a long line of tailors, being measured. Drill Sergeant Green stands with his glasses covering his eyes, politely asking us to move along. At the end of the line we are given four pairs of BDU bottoms; four pairs of BDU tops; one belt, black; one belt buckle, also black; four T-shirts, brown; four pairs of underwear, brown; four pairs of wool socks, olive drab green; two pairs of combat boots; two covers (what the rest of the world calls hats); two pairs of PT shorts, gray; and four PT shirts, gray.

We stuff all our clothing into a duffel bag and march to the PX, which is something like a military Wal-Mart. There we are told to buy running shoes, white socks, a combination lock, shaving cream, razors, foot powder, black shoe polish, soap, shampoo, shower shoes, stationery, stamps, writing utensils, and a phone card "in case anyone back home actually wants to hear from you."

Back at the barracks, we change into our BDUs. Drill Sergeant Green, who I am coming to understand is not so much a real drill sergeant as a liaison to help ease our transition into military life, explains the proper way to dress. The brown T-shirt is tucked in. The pants legs are tucked into the boots, and the boot laces are tucked into the boots as well. Boot laces that are not tucked in are called snakes. Snakes can earn you push-ups. Not having your brown T-shirt tucked in can earn you push-ups. Not wearing your cover the proper way can earn you push-ups. The BDU top is called a blouse. Calling it a shirt can earn you push-ups. We spend close to an hour learning the proper way to roll up the sleeves—rolling up your sleeves the wrong way can earn you push-ups—and after we have done this and donned our uniforms, we admire ourselves in the mirror. We strike poses and take on stern, soldierly faces, as if we will soon be called to war and now have to break the news to our girlfriends and mothers and fathers. We imagine our girlfriends weeping on some stone quay or tarmac somewhere, suddenly full of guilt that they haven't yet let us into their pants. We imagine our fathers solemnly offering a hand, our mothers trying to control their emotions.

Outside, we stand in formation before Drill Sergeant Green. "You privates look like D-O-D-O," he tells us, but we are wearing our uniforms now. We have made it through one whole morning in the army, and nothing, not even being told we look like shit, can dampen our indomitable spirits.

"Drill Sergeant, yes, Drill Sergeant," we say.

— — — ⸻ ⸻ — — — — — —

At chow, Smith, R., serves us mashed potatoes. He wears a hairnet and cook's whites and plastic gloves. When we come through in our uniforms he tells us we look like shit, but we have heard that one already. The marines we saw earlier are eating chow at the same time we are, and even though we are all in uniform now, there is a tangible difference between us.

The marines are relaxed, laughing and joking, and we are herded together like frightened cows. They laugh at us as we walk past them.

After chow we are marched to the post barbershop. We pay five dollars for a haircut that takes less than thirty seconds, and when we come out of the barbershop and stand in formation in our BDUs and our new haircuts, it is difficult to tell who is who, as if some basic sense of identity has been stolen from us. Later I will realize that this is exactly the case, that our identities have been taken away and we have been made uniform and equal. In the weeks to come, we will get haircuts every week, marched together as a platoon by our drill sergeant and stripped of what little hair has regrown since our last haircut. We will begin to sound the same, our voices hoarse from calling cadence and shouting answers to our drill sergeants. We will begin to use the same phrasing, the same words, and sometimes it will be difficult to tell where we end and someone else begins, but we do not know this now. We stand in the hot sun with our covers off, rubbing our heads over and over. Drill Sergeant Green smiles for the first time, revealing a gold tooth.

"You motherfuckers are high speed," he says. "You may make soldiers yet."

——— ——— ——— ——— ——— ——— ——— ——— ——— ——— ———

When Smith, R., comes back from KP he tells us that he fucked one of the women who serves food in the cafeteria line. We have only been away from home a few days but have seen no women except in the cafeteria line and a few women admin personnel who helped with the in-processing.

The women in the cafeteria are all at least two hundred years old. Smith, R., knows this, and we know that Smith, R., is full of heavy shit, but we are stuck in the barracks while night falls around us. Soon it will be lights-out and we will lie on our backs in the dark trying to ignore the solitary squeak of bedsprings that means a man is thinking of his girl back home.

So we listen to Smith, R. "You should of fucking seen it," he says and goes on to tell us in lurid detail about his encounter. He answers "Hell, yeah, man" and "Right there in the kitchen freezer" to our questions. I hear the phrase "golf ball through a garden hose" more than once.

Finally, Black calls bullshit. "They're, like, ninety," Black says. "You'd have to put two bags over her head, in case one of them tore. You'd have to put a bag over your own head, in case her two fell off. Even you wouldn't touch that shit."

Smith, R., confesses. "But," he says, holding up a finger, "after a few weeks with you fuckers even those bitches will start looking good."

"Not to me," Black says and tells us about his girl back home. We all have girls back home, and we smile a little at the remembrance, our eyes gone slightly glazed as Black says that he's getting married as soon as he gets back, that she is waiting for him, that they've dated since junior high. His eyes get a little teary as he tells us about her. He wipes at his cheek with the back of his hand while we look away, all except for Smith, R., who starts marching around the barracks calling cadences about Jody, the infamous lover who steals soldiers' girlfriends while they are off at training or war. After a few minutes we join Smith, R., marching in a long line around Black sitting on his bunk, twenty or thirty of us repeating his cadence:

Ain't no need in calling home,
Jody's on the telephone.
Ain't no need in going home,
Jody's got your girl and gone.

— — — — — — — — — —

We are woken at 0500. Smith, R., tells us the o stands for "Oh my God, it's fucking early," but no one joins in his laughter. To preserve our tight hospital corners, several of us slept on the floor, and once dressed, we climb back under our bunks and pretend to be tightening the corners while we go back to sleep until we are called for formation.

After chow we are marched to another anonymous building. Other recruits from other areas are already lined up outside, and through the grapevine we get the word: shots. Rumors pass up and down the line: The shots are for malaria and yellow fever because we are going to be sent to Panama after training. Or they are "just-in-case shots" because we are going to be given an off-base pass, and the shots are just in case we sleep with a prostitute. The shots are for AIDS and hepatitis and cancer. They are for the flu. Arthritis. Measles and mumps and rubella. Black says they are shots of saltpeter to keep our sex drives down, but Smith, R., says no, they put the saltpeter in the food.

Inside, the building smells of antiseptic and rubbing alcohol. At the door we sign our names and Social Security numbers and take off our blouses and roll up both sleeves of our T-shirts. We stand in a long line that moves slowly forward, each step punctuated by the sharp hiss. At the end of the line, four army doctors punch me with air guns like they're branding cattle. It is over in seconds. Four sharp stabs, almost simultaneous, and then we are protected against smallpox and measles and gonorrhea or whatever it is in the inoculations.

After the shots, we spend the morning standing in lines. In one line a doctor checks all our joints. Another doctor checks our eyesight. The next one checks our hearing. We are made to squat, to stand, to turn our heads and cough, to bend over and spread them. We are hit with rubber hammers to check our reflexes. We stick out our tongues. One doctor runs his scaly fingers inside our mouths and another shines a light in our ears, noses, and throats. Still another inspects us for lice and crabs.

Black is afraid when the doctors draw blood. "How much do they take?" he asks. We are standing in another line. We have been poked and prodded all morning and are now sore and tired and hungry. Ahead of us, more doctors are drawing blood into tiny vials. There is a rumor circulating that one guy passed out when they took his blood, but so far it is unsubstantiated. Black is nervous, fidgeting, looking as if he might pass out himself.

Smith, R., says they take a gallon.

"A gallon?" Black says, face going white.

Smith, R., shrugs. "We're being tested for AIDS. They have to take that much to get a good read."

Black looks as if he might bolt. "How do they know?" he says. "If you have AIDS? How do they know?"

Smith, R., shrugs again. "Your blood turns yellow right in front of everybody."

Drill Sergeant Green has crept up behind us. "You afraid you got the HIV, Black?"

"Drill Sergeant, no, Drill Sergeant," Black says, but we can see him thinking of everyone he has ever slept with, and when his blood does not turn yellow, he looks immensely relieved.

— — — — — — — — — —

The last thing we have to do with the doctors is piss in a cup. We all took a drug test when we were sworn in months before, but now we have to take another one. We are told that if we come forward and declare our drug use, we will be waived and allowed into the military anyway. Nothing will happen to us, we are assured, but no one believes it, even before Smith, R., tells us that it's a load of bullshit, that at best we will be unmercifully fucked with our entire time at Basic Training and, at worst, court-martialed.

We try to tell Black that your piss turns blue, but he's not going for it, although Perez, Smith, S., and Harris all look a little nervous. Smith, S., wonders aloud how long pot stays in your system.

"Years," Smith, R., tells him. "Fucking years and years. They can detect that shit a light-year from now."

We are taken in groups of four into the latrine, where an army doctor wearing rubber gloves hands us each a small cup and watches us fill it. After we fill it we hand it to the doctor, who seals it and then has us sign our name on our cup of urine so there can be no mistakes. Black claims he had to go so bad he filled twelve cups. Harris says he couldn't go with someone watching him, but the doctor wouldn't turn his back, so he stood there for close to thirty minutes before he could coax a small stream.

We never hear the results. We assume we all pass. Later we watch a film made especially for the military. In the film, soldiers stand in line waiting to be drug tested. The first soldier tells the camera how happy he is he has never used drugs. The second says he was offered some marijuana a few weeks ago but said no because he knew what it could do to his career.

The camera then pans to a goofy-looking soldier, an actor who you can tell has never been a soldier in his life. At first he looks surprised, then wistful, and finally saddened. He shakes his head, almost crying as he tells the camera, "Man, I wish I wouldn't have smoked that joint last night. I'm going to ruin my career. I'll be court-martialed and dishonorably discharged. My wife might leave me, and I could lose custody of my children. I wish I would have just said no."

For days we make fun of the film, repeating those last lines, but it isn't until later—when we are shipped to another part of the base to start training or perhaps even later than that, near the end, when the war begins—that we realize we are talking about our time in the military: that we might have just said no.

——— ——— ——— ——— ——— ——— ——— ——— ——— ——— ———

We are told that the shots may have a few side effects, such as fever, diarrhea, and/or vomiting. One recruit named Gregg decides to fake the symptoms. He has been complaining the entire time we've been at Reception Station. At night, he tells anyone who will listen that he made a serious mistake. He joined the army because he needed the money and there weren't any jobs where he's from. He is one of many who are in the same position—no job, no prospects for a future. The rest of us are here for college money, joining the reserves or the National Guard to pay for our education, and we know that after Basic we are going home, where we'll serve one weekend a month. For us it is only the three months of Basic we have to survive. For the others, those who are Regular Army, it is years and years. Some soldiers have enlisted for six years and may not see their parents or friends or girlfriends for two. They might be shipped overseas, to Germany or Korea or any of the myriad military bases scattered around the world.

So, like Gregg, some of them are trying to get out. Johnson has been limping for the last two days. So far he has not complained, but we see him take on pained expressions each time Drill Sergeant Green is near. His limp becomes more pronounced by the hour. This morning, when he stumbled and almost fell in front of Green, the drill sergeant lowered his sunglasses.

"What in the hell is the matter with you, dumbass?"

Johnson struck a grimace, his hand going to his lower back. "I think I hurt my back real bad, Drill Sergeant."

Drill Sergeant Green raised his sunglasses. "Rub some dirt on it," he said and went on.

We all know Gregg is faking. Drill Sergeant Green calls him Pepto-Bismol. He refuses to let Gregg out of formation when he complains that he is going to vomit or that he has diarrhea. Drill Sergeant Green tells him to let it run down his leg. Gregg stands hopping from one foot to the other. At night, he leans over the toilet making retching sounds. We tell him to shut the fuck up before he gets our asses in some heavy shit. Watching him, I think that he must want out of the army pretty bad to fake diarrhea and vomiting for days on end. Then, later, I wonder if it will work.

——— ——— ——— ——— ——— ——— ——— ——— ——— ———

All of us have seen *Full Metal Jacket*. At night, we discuss scenes in the movie. We compare R. Lee Ermey to Drill Sergeant

Green. Smith, R., says Drill Sergeant Green would kick the shit out of R. Lee Ermey, but no one agrees with him.

No one talks about the second part of the movie, the Vietnam part, except to quote the Vietnamese prostitute who says, "Me love you long time." Instead, we focus on the training part, where R. Lee Ermey stalks around with a permanent scowl on his face, hitting Vincent D'Onofrio's character when he can't tell his left from his right. We tell Harris, who is from Texas, that the only things that come from Texas are steers and queers and Harris doesn't have any horns. Smith, R., says Black is a disgusting fatbody, and Black tells Smith, R., that he is a slimy scumbag puke piece of shit.

We have also seen *Biloxi Blues* and *An Officer and a Gentleman* and *Stripes*—any movie having anything to do with Basic Training, as if by watching movies we could understand what it would be like. As if by watching movies of war one could understand what war is like. We never talk about the Vietnam part of the movie because, as Smith, R., puts it, "I ain't going to no fucking war. When this shit is over, I'm going fucking home."

— — — — — — — — — — — —

We are told early on that there is no color in the army, but despite the lack of color, or the only color being green—the drill sergeants use both phrases—the barracks are segregated. I do not mean that white and black soldiers sleep in different barracks but that we subconsciously segregate ourselves, aligning ourselves by race. We are told over and over that we are a team that must learn to work together if we are to survive. When the drill sergeants are watching, we are. But at night we isolate ourselves in different ends of the barracks, with a few empty bunks in the center as a sort of buffer zone.

Smith, R., despite having a father and three brothers in the military, is an unabashed racist. But his father has told him the military is changing, and, as Smith, R., puts it one night, "they can run your ass out just for thinking the word 'nigger.'"

He stops and looks around, sighing as if he'd been asked to donate a kidney. "That'd be some heavy motherfucking shit, wouldn't it?"

I think of explaining to Smith, R., exactly how many things are wrong with those two comments, but Smith, R., has taken off his thick glasses. Without them his eyes are weak. He squints toward the far end of the barracks. He looks somehow vulnerable without his glasses on, like a slug that has just had salt poured on it.

When he puts his glasses back on he is smiling. "When's the last time you got any pussy?" he says. "Hey, you ever fuck a black girl?"

—　—　—　—　—　—　—　—　—　—

We spend our days waiting. This is part and parcel of military procedure. I will hear the term "hurry up and wait" a hundred times in the next few days. We wait in line for chow. We wait in line to use the latrine. We wait in line at the post exchange, at the post office, at the barbershop. We wait standing in formation. We wait inside the barracks. We wait for Sunday so we can go to chapel and escape training for an hour. We wait for nightfall, for the darkness of the barracks, so we can be alone with our thoughts.

We fill out vast amounts of paperwork. We sign waivers of all kinds. We sign bank deposit slips and traveler's checks. We sign over and over, not even looking at what we are signing. We could be signing away our firstborn children or signing our bodies to medical research. We could be signing that we hate the United States of America, that we are communists or anarchists or terrorists. We sign our name and Social Security number again and again. We relate our next of kin, whom to notify in case of emergency, which makes me wonder what kinds of emergencies have occurred in the past.

We are issued identification cards and told to keep them on us at all times. We are issued dog tags with our name, date of birth, blood type, and religious preference. We are told that during battle, soldiers wear one tag around their neck and one around their right toe, so that if they are blown to pieces their disparate parts can still be identified, which makes me wonder aloud what happens if several soldiers are blown to pieces and the pieces all land in one large pile or if their toe tags are blown so far from their neck tags that no one recovers them.

Perez says we could be hit with napalm or some other flammable substance and the heat would blacken our tags to the point they are unreadable. Ebel says we could be run over by a tank, the treads mangling our tags. Harris says we could be shot once in the toe and once in the chest, the two shots cleanly eviscerating our identifying information, and for the rest of the day we concoct scenarios in which our bodies are never identified, the simplest being that, while on R&R, a pickpocket or prostitute steals them, thinking they are jewelry, and the worst being somehow, while on patrol, being attacked and eaten by sea lions.

Often when we are waiting, we are given details. There are dozens of details a soldier in Basic Training can be assigned. Latrine detail is scouring the toilet with industrial-grade Comet and wiping down the mirrors and mopping with some form of military Pine-Sol, which, instead of a lemony fresh smell leaves a smell like a combination of stomach virus and rubbing alcohol. When everything has been wiped down, the latrine must look like it has never been used, even though after each meal it is flooded because, as Smith, R., puts it, "you pick up a load, you drop off a load."

KP is called "kitchen police," a common detail in the military where soldiers work for the day helping the kitchen staff. After his first morning on KP, Smith, R., tells us it sucks ass. He says he stood slopping mashed potatoes onto marines' trays all morning, that the marines knew he was a new recruit and so fucked with him unmercifully, blowing kisses at him, telling him how cute he was. After lunch he worked in the washroom, where a huge stainless steel machine farted and belched and steamed the plastic trays. He had to wear a trash bag with holes for neck and arms cut out, he got soaked anyway, his glasses steamed up, and he burned all the skin off his hands.

"I didn't enlist to work in a fucking kitchen," he says.

There is also "policing" the grounds for trash, cigarette butts, or dog doo—anything that might offend a passing officer. Two or three days a week, depending on whether any visiting dignitaries are in the area, a hundred or so soldiers are detailed to mow, to sweep up the mown grass, and to trim any hedges, trees, or shrubs that have gotten unruly in the last week.

Brass detail is policing all the spent brass at the rifle range. Fireguard is a two-hour shift in the middle of the night to watch for fires. CQ is charge of quarters, which to new recruits means the same thing as fireguard: less sleep.

But despite our high-speed uniforms and our military haircuts, it is hard to feel good about being a soldier when you are picking up bird shit because a second lieutenant might someday walk by or when, after scrubbing the toilet for forty-five minutes, your drill sergeant comes in and lowers his trousers, and the only thing you can do is hope that the industrial-strength Comet will eat away his ass cheeks.

— — — — — — — — — — —

After we have been given haircuts and issued uniforms, after all our shots have been injected, in the long periods of downtime we have, we take classes. We are just waiting now for enough new recruits to arrive at Reception Station to fill a new battalion for Basic Training, and the classes are a brief introduction to what we will learn when the real training begins.

We learn the basics of drill and ceremony, the movements and marching. How to stand at attention, parade rest, at ease. We learn how to salute. We learn how to polish our boots. We learn our three general orders and how to do a proper push-up.

We learn the chain of command, starting with the president and vice-president, going all the way down through the base commander and our battalion commander and our drill sergeant. We learn rank and insignia, the difference between an officer and an NCO, a private and a corporal, a general and a colonel.

We learn military rules and punishments, what happens when a recruit's infractions cannot be disciplined with push-ups. One soldier is given an Article 15 for eating a candy bar—besides the stiff fine docked from his paycheck, he has to guard the candy machine for three hours a night. He is given a rubber M16 and forced to march three steps back and forth before it, warning away any soldier who might draw near.

Later, we will learn to be soldiers: how to stab someone with a bayonet, how to fire an M16, an M60, an M203 grenade launcher. We will learn to dig foxholes, to throw hand grenades, to camouflage our faces and our hands and our rifles. We will learn how to use the radio to call down artillery strikes, how to don our gas masks in case of chemical attack, how to inject ourselves with antidote.

But for now we learn rules and regulations, to pay attention to detail, to clean toilets and ladle mashed potatoes. We learn to walk, to wear our uniforms, to stand and talk in a new way, because part of being a soldier is relearning everything the military way because there is no other way to do it.

We learn to march because marching makes us move as one unit. We learn drill and ceremony because everything must be done down to the finest detail. We learn to scrub toilets because our world must be as clean and precise as possible, and we learn to jump when our drill sergeants say "frog" because, in the military, absolute and unquestioning discipline is required, and if it is not received your world will become a place filled with shit.

And we learn the language, because military doctrine is steeped in language, and one cannot understand the military without understanding the language it uses.

It is the language of the acronym. To leave without permission is to be AWOL. Anyone who goes AWOL is subject to the UCMJ. Your job is your MOS. ASAP means right away. ETS is when you are allowed to leave the service, though in some cases you might be IRR and can still be activated in case of war. There's also KP, D and C, FTX, and BRM. There's BC, BDU, and BCT. There's CO, CQ, and NBC. There's IG, KIA, MIA, MOPP, MP, MRE, MLRS, and NCO. There's POV and POW. PT and PX. SOP, SITREP, and XO. RnR, SNAFU, and SOS.

It is the language of the metaphor. Chow is food. Jody is the guy who is sleeping with your girlfriend while you are away—Suzy is usually the girlfriend. A restroom is a latrine. Yesterday means the same thing as ASAP, as in "I want it done yesterday." Squared away means up to military regulation, someone who has everything in order. Ate up means stupid, unsquared away, as in "He's ate up with the dumbass." Someone not ate up with the dumbass is high speed, as in "high speed, low drag," or squared away. The ugly eyeglasses issued in the military are BCGs, or birth-control glasses. D-O-D-O spells doo-doo.

It is the language of the nasty nickname. Bumfuck is an isolated location. A cheesedick is a suck-up, a radio is a prick. Your sleeping bag is a fart sack. Any male in the military is a swinging dick. In World War II, the Germans were Krauts, and the Japanese were slopes. In Vietnam, the Vietnamese were called slopes, dinks, or gooks. By the end of Basic, when the war begins, the Iraqis are towel heads and sand niggers. The military is an equal opportunity employer, however, and is often derogatory toward its own. NAVY: Never Again Volunteer Yourself. MARINE: Muscles Are Required, Intelligence Not Essential. ARMY: Ain't Ready for Marines Yet. Air force: chair force.

It is also the language of the euphemism. Front-leaning rest is push-up position. Retrograde advance is a retreat. The front line is now called the forward edge of battle area. Boots are called leather personnel carriers. A rectal cranial inversion is to have one's head up one's ass. A blanket party (immortalized in

Full Metal Jacket) is when soldiers beat an unpopular soldier or one who continually causes punishment by being ate up with the dumbass, an unsquared-away soldier who usually wears BCGs and cries about his ETS being so far away, who wishes he could go AWOL because Jody is at his house, who hates PT and D and C and KP, who will never re-up because he hates everything about the army and would do anything to just go home.

It is a language where weapons of mass destruction become weapons of mass destruction program–related activities once weapons of mass destruction are not found. Where someone who is sick is called a broke-dick, soldiers new to a unit are "fucking new guys," women soldiers are called cleaning barrels, and anything that doesn't go according to SOP is a clusterfuck, a SNAFU, a monkey fucking a football. Where "conflict" replaces the word "war" and "collateral damages" replaces "civilian casualties." Where war is declared against anything we disagree with, from drugs to poverty and terrorism, because, in military language, declaring war against intangible and abstract ideas is the ultimate metaphor.

— — — — — — — — — — —

Just before we ship from Reception Station to our Basic Training area, we are given the luxury of watching a movie. We have received our shots. We are dressed properly, our hair clipped to military regulations. We know our three general orders and our chain of command and the difference between a general and a private. We know how to march, how to stand at attention, parade rest, at ease. We are high speed, at least as high speed as we can get at Reception Station.

We crowd into an auditorium with two or three hundred other new arrivals, some of them just off the bus, still in civilian clothes. Two of the new recruits have long hair and earrings, and we fuck with them unmercifully. Dornan finds dried wads of gum beneath the seats and beans them in the back of the head, and Black keeps leaning over the seat telling one of them how cute he is, how he reminds Black of his girlfriend back home. He says she likes it up the ass and he misses her terribly and he doesn't know if he can make it much longer without fucking something. Black is over six feet tall and weighs close to 250, and every time he makes a kissing noise the long-haired recruit flinches. When Black casually puts a hand on his shoulder, the recruit begins crying, and when he begins crying, Smith, R., tells him that fucking shit ain't going to work with none of these motherfuckers around this fucking place, so he can just dry that stupid shit right the fuck up.

The movie is *The Green Berets*. John Wayne. America. Red, white, and blue. *With silver wings upon their chest. These are the men, America's best. One hundred men will test today, but only three win the Green Beret.* In the movie, John Wayne is a colonel commanding a company of Green Berets from Fort Bragg. Their mission is to secure a new base camp in Vietnam nicknamed Dodge City. The Green Berets are elite special forces—they are trained in every aspect of warfare. They speak several languages each. They carry M16s and M14s and grenade launchers, and their gunships fire air-to-land rockets and .30-caliber machine guns, but we like their tight haircuts and their green berets.

We watch as John Wayne and his men reinforce the camp, as the Vietcong murder and maim villagers in the camp's surrounding area, villagers that the American soldiers have been trying to protect. We watch as the VC overrun Dodge City after a battle that lasts all night, and we cheer when, in the morning, John Wayne calls in Puff the Magic Dragon and the gunship lays waste to the Vietcong. When John Wayne cuts down the communist flag the VC have run up the flagpole, we wish we wore silver wings on our chests, that we were Army Rangers with years of training and green berets.

In a few days, we will get on a bus and ride to the 6000 area, where we will spend the next three months. We will meet drill sergeants who dedicate their lives to acting like R. Lee Ermey in *Full Metal Jacket*. Our drill sergeants will be the first thing we see in the morning and the last thing we see at night, and we will come to understand that we say "Drill Sergeant, yes, Drill Sergeant" because our world begins and ends with our drill sergeants. We will fire M16s and M60s and M203 grenade launchers. We will throw hand grenades, set off claymore mines, crawl through barbed wire with tracer fire streaking overhead and concussion grenades going off all around us, but most of the time it will be more of the same: swapping stories of women back home, getting our bunks and our lockers and our shower shoes squared away. Quoting military movies that romanticize training, romanticize war and killing and death. Standing in line and filling out paperwork, KP and D and C and PT, because that, we will come to understand, is what the army is: rules and regulations, long lines, dumbfuck details and waiting to go home or be shipped somewhere around the world, where we will wait for a war to break out or wait to be shipped back home.

In August Saddam Hussein will invade Kuwait and the U.S. Army will begin mobilizing for the mother of all wars. Many of the men I am in Basic with will be shipped overseas to kill—or be killed.

But for now we cheer. We cheer because we are told to cheer, because for this one moment, as the theme song from *The Green Berets* plays in our heads and we march in lockstep together, we are soldiers.

"You motherfuckers love this man's army?" Drill Sergeant Green yells.

"Drill Sergeant, yes, Drill Sergeant," we say.

NO GO

Fredericks failed the gas chamber and got a no go, so he had to circle back through. When he failed the second time—unable to stand the smoke, the burning on his hands and eyes, the vomiting—he was recycled, a word that means, in military terms, that he had to start over, not just the gas chamber but all of Basic Training.

The same thing happened to half a dozen at the rifle range and another handful on the PT test near the end—they were no goes because they couldn't shoot or run fast enough or stand the smoke when their masks were off, so they were failed, stopped, recycled, sent back. No go.

Even in the morning we were no goed, or maybe the correct verb is no went. I don't know, just like I didn't know what was happening when I woke in the morning to a darkness that wouldn't stop coming for another three hours, drill sergeants stalking up and down the barracks telling soldiers their bunks were no goes and their boots were no goes and their goddamn fucking attitude was a fucking no go. All of us were no goes because we didn't know what we were doing, the words "no no, fuck no" floating around us at all times, like cartoon bubbles or the measured tread of boots.

Certain places were no goes as well. The common room was a no go because we weren't allowed to watch TV or relax on the couches for even a moment. We couldn't go in the latrine after it had been cleaned in the morning, which meant it was a no go even if we had to go. We couldn't wash the tiredness out of our eyes, the redness from crying or lack of sleep caused by the knowing we'd be here so long we might never go home.

We weren't allowed in the armory where our weapons were kept, and we weren't allowed downrange during firing. We weren't allowed anywhere near the live-fire bunkers or the distant fields where artillery shouted all day and night. We weren't allowed in any other part of the base except for mornings, when we ran through the darkness with only streetlights to guide us, past the tanks and artillery, past the batteries of other soldiers also running, their voices as hoarse as ours, like hound dogs or hurricanes, circling endlessly every morning the streets of Fort Sill, Oklahoma, past MP jeeps waiting to track down any soldier who peeled off from the platoon and tried to go home.

We weren't allowed to speak to old recruits when we were new or new recruits when we were old. We couldn't talk to the marines also stationed there, though they talked to us, shouting how much shit we had signed on for. We weren't allowed to speak to the civilians who worked on base except to say "size nine" if they asked what size shoe we wore or "no, sir" if they asked if that was too tight. Same with the civilians at the PX we weren't allowed to go into or the old men at the barbershop who shaved our heads in seven seconds.

We weren't allowed to read. Not newspapers our parents sent us, not books, not the Bible. Maybe we just didn't have time and I'm remembering this wrongly, but I'm also sure that news from the outside world might have interrupted our training, and so it was banned, named no go. Books might have made us think about what we were doing, as they did for me years later when I read *The Sun Also Rises* and *The Things They Carried* and *Redeployment*. The Bible might have made us put our faith in God instead of our drill sergeants, and newspapers might have told us about the forces stirring in the Middle East.

We couldn't go in the barracks during the heat of the day. We couldn't go inside the CQ, or the BC's office, or the quartermaster's, not if we needed TP for the barracks or PT uniforms for our bodies or stationery to write a letter back home asking if someone could come get us. We couldn't go outside our drill area, not to the mess hall or the canteen. We weren't allowed to use the phones except on Sunday, and then we stood in a long line waiting to hear the voices of our mothers and fathers, who always told us to keep going.

——— ——— ——— ——— ——— ——— ——— ——— ——— ——— ———

Most mornings we did nothing but march. In a parking lot beside the barracks we spun in big round wheels under the just-rising sun, fifty men trying, and failing, to move together. At noon we went to the mess hall and then back to the parking lot after chow, where we circled until we could feel the concrete beneath the floors of our black boots and our legs trembled from all the turns. The sun stabbed down like a spear. In a brief moment in the shade, someone would moan that the drills sergeants meant to kill us, which was only another way of saying we would march until we could not go anymore, none of us realizing we had not gone anywhere all day except around an empty parking lot.

In the late evening—the sun just setting and the horizon turned to fire—we ran the same two-mile circle, drill sergeants eyeing their stopwatches as we went by, saying, "No go, no go, no go, fuck no." We had to work together on these evening runs so everyone made time, but always someone, no matter how hard we pushed him, could not keep up. We had to keep circling then, and afterward we'd hurl angry words at whoever held us up, saying, "Fuck you, you fucking no go," already adopting the language of our oppressors.

Through all of June we were sent to the rifle range in cattle cars that rattled as we rode. We unloaded as if we had finally arrived somewhere worth being, but all we did was lie in the dirt for twenty days and learn to fire our rifles. After the first day, we dreaded going. We liked the live-fire shooting targets of Soviet soldiers, but most of the time we were only waiting, trying to find some shade out of the sun, wondering where we would be sent next. When we graduated two months later, some of my fellow soldiers would go to the Middle East as the first Gulf War kicked up, and when the second one began ten years later it would occur to me that the soldier is always being sent somewhere, then being told to go back, to go here, to not go, no go, fuck no, now go. Because of this type of training, all the soldier ever wants to do is go home. Or in some cases, go back.

———— —— —— —— —— —— —— —— —— —— ——

There were among us in those early days a couple of men who wanted out of the army so badly they became permanent no goes. One guy developed a back problem. Another limped everywhere, though he didn't limp when he thought no one was looking and sometimes limped on the wrong leg. Rumor had it one soldier had tried to injure himself by tying a buffer cord around his neck and throwing the buffer out the window, but he miscalculated the length of the cord and only broke the buffer.

Their idea was to leave. These were men who had enlisted for six years and after only a week decided they had made the wrong decision. They could not take the long days or the physical exercise or the mental conditioning. They thought they could get out of the army by faking an injury but instead were put on light duty. They walked around all day picking up trash or were put on permanent kitchen duty, where they scrubbed pots and pans and came home with burns on their hands from the hot water.

We called them broke-dicks, as if the penis is a symbol of manhood and these were not men. As if the first thing to break in a man is not his spirit but his cock, and he must walk around holding it because it's weak and ineffectual, broken, no go.

All day, as we marched around the hot parking lots or crowded into cattle cars, we'd see these broke-dicks wandering slowly around the grounds looking for trash or waiting for the bus that would take them to the mess hall. I still wonder when it occurred to them that they were never getting out. Paperwork is slow in the army, but they were there long after I left, which means they spent months doing nothing. I imagine the days passed so slowly they wondered what they were doing, or maybe they thought they could beat the military and would eventually be released, their files stamped with No Go, which would mean, of course, that they could go.

My best guess is they were eventually recycled. Sent back to the beginning. The military does not like to release those who have sworn in. Despite the number of no goes in training, there's no getting out, not for a fake limp or a back problem or a broken buffer cord. Not for failure at the rifle range or the gas chamber or with a hand grenade. There's only recycling. I hate to think they spent six years picking up trash, so I say they eventually toughened their resolve and sucked up whatever fears they'd been holding inside, finally realizing there's no such thing as a no go to get out. In the military, we always did whatever we were doing again and again and again, no matter the consequences. There's no way out. Only forward. Only go.

— — — — — — — — — — —

Other things that were recycled besides soldiers: our M16s, which were from the Vietnam era, a thing we talked about during the endless days of the rifle range, wondering whether the weapons we were holding had ever killed anyone; most of our gear, including helmets, rucksacks, E-tools, and canteens, which we carried with us at all times because in the heat of summer not drinking water was a no go that could get you dead; bedsheets and wool blankets and sleeping bags that never kept us warm at night because we never slept long enough to get warm; the barracks where thousands had gone before us and thousands more would go after; the base itself, recycled from land stolen from Mexico, who stole it from Spain, who stole it from Indigenous tribes; the idea that breaking men down made them stronger once they were built back up; gas masks and MOPP gear and gloves, without which you could not escape the gas chamber, the thing that started all this, thinking of Fredericks failing and the drill sergeants screaming as Fredericks vomited. "That's a no go, private," one drill sergeant shouted, while another gathered Fredericks's snot on a stick. He was holding a contest to see who had the most snot coming out of their gas masks and he held up Fredericks's offering with admiration while Fredericks tried to suck in great lungfuls of clean air, already knowing he'd have to go back inside if he wanted to pass, the drill sergeant with his stick saying, "That's a winner, Fredericks. You might be a no go, but your snot here wins."

—   —   —   —   —   —   —   —   —   —   —

Other things we threw away, such as the names of the men we served alongside. I remember Alarid and Talley and Keller and Perez, Benavidez and Biobaku and Buist, Ebel and Ordendorff and Fowler. Kale and Diamond and Pena and Ramirez and Sykes and Smith, so maybe I've only thrown away the memory of the days when I could not stand some of them, when the heat or the tiredness or the anger got inside me, like the day Palmer pushed me too far and I raised the butt of my rifle right about the time the drill sergeant walked in. He saw me and shook his head and I spent the rest of the night with my rifle raised until my arms shook, a team of drill sergeants circling around me, saying, "That's a goddamn no go."

—   —   —   —   —   —   —   —   —   —   —

Another form of no go would be that the United States never left Japan or Germany. We still have military bases in both countries, as well as in Korea and Vietnam and the islands we accrued from Spain. We've never left the Middle East, either, not if we're mentioning bases or military presence, which leads me to believe that "no go" has never applied to whoever has the most force. The United States has bases in 150 countries, whether they want us there or not, whether we've been told to go, to which we must have said, "No, no, fuck no."

— — — — — — — — — — —

During the Gulf Wars, the Department of Defense instituted a no go for all soldiers. It was called stop loss, but what it meant was no go. No one was allowed to leave the military during the war, not those with a minute or a month left of their service. They could be kept where they were in Kabul or Tikrit or called up at any time and shipped overseas. They could be held indefinitely here in the states, always on alert, neither going nor staying.

Because of stop loss, many units have served multiple tours in Iraq and Afghanistan. Some tours get extended by six months, then another six. Some soldiers come home for a few months and are shipped back, and I always wonder how they wake in the morning knowing they must go back, if they think, No no fuck no. If they think about service. Salvation. What it means to be a soldier. If they only want to sleep for a few more minutes, or months.

— — — — — — — — — — —

Roughly twenty U.S. Armed Forces veterans commit suicide every day. In 2014, the latest year statistics are available, almost 7,400 veterans took their own lives. From 2001, when the United States invaded Afghanistan, to 2014, the suicide rate for female military service members rose 85 percent. The rate for men rose 40 percent. One in four active service members shows signs of a mental health condition, including post-traumatic stress disorder, depression, and traumatic brain injury.

Among veterans, one in three develop mental problems within three to four months of being home. One in five turn to heavy drinking or drugs. The rate of depression for veterans is five times higher than for civilians. The rate for intermittent explosive disorder, which results in episodes of extreme anger, is six times higher. The rate for PTSD is fifteen times higher.

Some veterans miss the structure that the military life provides. Some miss feeling a sense of purpose in their daily work. Some of them come back unaccustomed to silence, so they explode in anger. Some come back missing the months or years they were gone, the parts of their children's lives they can never have, or the nights they lay awake under different stars and wondered how hard their wife or husband or mother or father were worrying about them. Some soldiers come back missing limbs. Some come back missing lives. All of them come back missing some small part of them, whether it be fingers or a foundation on which to stand or an understanding of how the world makes sense anymore.

Those who do return often feel isolated because civilians don't understand the experience of serving. Of seeing friends die. Of seeing bodies staring sightless at the blue sky on the arm of an unnamed mountain. How a man can wish he had never gone at the same time he wishes he would never return.

Of the 1.7 million soldiers who have served in Iraq and Afghanistan, 300,000 suffer from PTSD or depression. That's roughly how many U.S. soldiers fought, total, in the Spanish-American War and the War of 1812. It's the number of non-battle deaths in all U.S. wars combined, which means that although the bombs or bullets didn't get them, something else did.

It also means that all of them, every single one, would be declared no go. Unfit for military service, now that their service is done. Which means it was the service that made them no go and not the other way around.

At its heart, no go means to fail. That the soldier cannot continue until he qualifies, but to be unable to continue, of course, can also mean to be hurt. Injured or ill, sent to sick call, where we said he was broke-dick or broken down, and when a soldier is broken down he is relieved from all duty. He cannot keep going, not to war or anywhere.

No go can also mean he is not good enough. Not strong enough, or fast enough, or just not enough. Many who return from war believe they were not strong enough or fast enough to save the soldiers they saw fall beside them, and so they consider themselves no goes. They stop at that moment of their life when they believe they failed and never move past it. They are trying, again and again, to qualify. To be found passing.

It can mean wounded in spirit as well as body. To sit alone in a room with a bottle and stare into the abyss its mouth makes as the shadows move on the wall. To wake and not have the strength to get out of bed or to walk alone at night through the dark parts of the heart, seeing things marked no go that won't go away no matter how they're marked.

It can mean stasis. To stay in the same place. Stopped altogether or spinning like the stars in the night sky.

— — — — — — — — — — —

When the first Gulf War began, most of us thought we were going because we were told so every morning.

"Even all the broke-dicks and no goes," one drill sergeant said, standing on the drill pad at oh dark thirty, our eyes red from two months of lack of sleep, voices hoarse as the night surrounding us.

Overnight, our definition of no go shifted from worrying about how to best polish our boots to worrying about war, thinking we would be sent from the rifle ranges in western Oklahoma to the open range of the desert. From the distant artillery rounds of Fort Sill to the Scud missiles of Saddam Hussein. From the gas chamber to the gas chamber. Most of us couldn't find Kuwait on a map, and late at night we'd wonder whether that marked us as no go.

"I haven't qualified yet," Ordendorff said, and Fredericks nodded, practicing with his gas mask. We knew by then that Hussein had chemical weapons, and each night we waited for the drill sergeants to toss a smoke grenade into the barracks to test us. We needed to be tested, needed to know if we could pass. For weeks we had been wondering if we could even make it through training, if we were strong enough and fast enough and smart enough to be soldiers. Now we were being told we would be soldiers for real, with all the bullets and bombs that entails, so all that night we lay awake wondering.

"When do you think we'll go?" Alarid asked, but no one could answer, the same as when he asked if anyone was afraid.

In the morning, we hadn't slept. We were always tired, but now we were scared. We stood in the darkness waiting until the drill sergeants came out. On the big bulletin board had been written the latest news from the Middle East, all the divisions and deployments, but we were already so tired we could hardly stand. The drill sergeants stood before us in their mirrored shades and stared, and we all knew we were being weighed. We wondered whether we'd be found wanting or worthy. We didn't know what either meant. Of course we didn't. Our only tests had been in the safety of training. There were bullets fired at us, but they were blank. We spent too much time marching in place. The only bombs we had ever heard were too far away to worry us, and here we were, on the threshold of the unknown.

The drill sergeants called us to attention. "Let's go, then," they said, and we went off, wondering whether we were boarding an airplane or only beating around in our boots.

——— ——— ——— ——— ——— ——— ——— ——— ——— ——— ———

Sometimes I wake from dreams of being back in the military and reach for my notebook to capture the images, but they're already gone, leaving me with only a fleeting feeling of fear. What I wonder when I wake late at night, or sit at my computer in the early morning remembering Alarid and Talley and Sykes and Buist, is whether I am less a soldier for not having gone to war. Because my National Guard unit had recently switched from an evac hospital to an air-defense artillery unit, we were deemed unfit for service during the Gulf War. We were no goes because not enough of us had qualified in our new jobs, so we watched the war from home, always wondering what we would have done, how we would have fared in the battlegrounds under a sky bent with bombs.

So I keep circling, trying to ascertain if passing through the gas chamber would have prepared me for the sarin gas that never came in the Gulf. If raising a rifle at a target is the same as raising one at an enemy. I wonder what I would have done if I would have been found a soldier who served solidly. I keep asking questions about the military, about civilians who say "thank you for your service" without understanding what that service meant. I keep trying to understand what service is, if it means circling around the subject without ever asking for answers, or if it means diving into the dark heart of the questions we rarely ask.

I wonder whether the wars we fight are for freedom. If we keep going because that's where we've always gone. I wonder if that makes me a no go. I worry Buist would beat my ass for asking. Or maybe Sykes would say that yes, he'd been feeling the same thing, that he's not a damn bit freer than he was before all the wars began. I wonder what it means that we were young kids being told again and again we were no goes, then being told to go, to fight for the freedom of another country and claim it as ours.

In all our training we only circled around. On long marches we always came back to the barracks, then started again the next day. So, too, do our wars circle back. The First World War circled into the second, same as the wars we've been fighting in the Gulf. I suspect we will be there forever, the same as we've been in Germany and Japan and Korea. As if we've never learned anything. As if we are always saying "thank you for your service," always standing on a tarmac seeing bodies brought out the backs of airplanes. Always wondering what we would have done, those of us who woke one morning to the news we might have to go, who secretly hoped we would be found wanting because the fear of failure is weaker than the fear of death.

When the hammer came down, we all wanted out—out of the army, out of the coming war. We might have entertained the image of ourselves storming bunkers and defusing bombs, but what we really wanted was to be declared no go so we could excuse ourselves, say it was flat feet and not fear that kept us out of combat. Late at night we contemplated failing our last PT test, even though it meant we'd be stuck here indefinitely, because indefinite was better than dead. I still want out of the feeling that I should have been fired at, of the anger I have at people who say "thank you for your service" but never say a word after, as if thanks is all we need to give. I want out of the idea that I'm more a man for having been in the military, out of the belief that we fight for freedom, out of a country who thinks a single sentence serves as salve for the things our soldiers have seen.

One night near the end of training we were told to expect an attack. This was FTX, field training exercise, where we played at war, but after almost a week we were so tired we could not keep our eyes open. We'd been up for three days and were supposed to keep watch, but none of us could stay awake. When the attack came we were still asleep. The drill sergeants threw flashbangs and then came through with their rifles on rock and roll. They had popped gas, and smoke rolled through our foxholes, and by the time we came awake we were already dead, drill sergeants saying, as they always did, no go, no go, no go.

CADENCE

Each morning began with military music, speakers mounted on flagpoles playing reveille, and from a deep sleep of dreams not about this place, we heard the horns. Then came the quick switch of lights and fluorescents flickering overhead, accompanied by the crash of something thrown, a trash can or gas canister. The voices of the drill sergeants rose out of the chaos, and we fell from bed to the floor and tried to sleep for another two seconds under our bunks until the black boots came crushing down the aisles and forced us to rise.

We ran to the latrine then, our new song the turn of taps and rush of running water. The fluids and flatulences, the scrubbing of teeth, the groans and grimaces as new aches arose on our beaten-down bodies. This was Basic Training, and there were always new injuries announcing themselves as we woke and prepared ourselves for the day, our bodies like tired old men, our pain another part of the song we heard each morning, whines and cries joining with the farts and shouts of "fuck" as we tried to rouse ourselves.

We dressed staring at the darkness out the windows, silent now but for the rustle of clothing and our low curses about what was to come. When we had finished dressing, our lockers slammed closed together and our feet hammered the stairs in rhythm as we rushed down to the drill pad. The air lay thick and heavy in summer, Fort Sill, Oklahoma, 1990, just before the war began, but we didn't know that then, only that a long day lay ahead of us and here was only the beginning.

The streetlights were still on and the air smelled of bitterweed and heat as we stretched on the concrete, calling cadence, our voices echoing beneath the big building. Our drill sergeants' voices hung hoarse in the hot morning, and our own voices came harsh as hounds over the hill as we finished stretching and marched to the road for our morning run. All up and down the area other batteries were doing the same, and already the voices rose like a choir, calling cadence softly into the coming morning, the fading night.

In the early morning rain,
in the early morning rain.
In the early morning ra-a-a-ain,
in the early morning rain.

— — — — — — — — — — —

And so we sang, the sky lit up not with light but with litany, a thousand or ten thousand voices all calling cadence out of the darkness. Flashlights bobbed and weaved along the road outside the barracks buildings, vast edifices drawn into shape now by the yellow lights ringing them all around. The sun had not yet come up and the air still felt heavy and there was a pit of fear forming in our stomachs at what lay ahead, but for a time there was the song to focus on. While calling cadence we could forget about everything else: the future, friends and family, what forces were at work in the world.

We started slow, still marching, singing about the early morning rain, about going off to fight a war, a common old cadence, one we sang every morning in the darkness before dawn drew the world into familiar forms. As we marched, the dark shapes of other batteries moved past, men just awoken from sleep now singing of cold hills in foreign countries, the desolation and destruction of war, the loneliness and despair that can creep into a soldier far from home. Fort Sill felt like a foreign country on those hot mornings, Perez and Talley and Ramirez and Buist marching beside me, each of us looking at the others with something like kinship, or at least the common bond men in uniform share, men who are forced to suffer through such conditions.

Already our T-shirts were soaked, sweat springing up on our shaved heads. Already the sides of the road were littered with men doing push-ups and sit-ups and jumping jacks, then sprinting to catch up with their platoons. Already the voices were deep throated as despair, and were it not for the songs we sang, we might have given into despair.

Just past the next barracks the call came for double time and we took off, the cadence rising now, quicker, the flashlights passing like searchlights at sea. We did not know how far we would run each morning, whether a mile or ten miles, only that we had to keep up, to lock our bodies into the rhythm of the run, to focus on the cadence to get us through. The first gray glow lit the far horizon and a thousand voices raised themselves in song. Our feet hammered the road, creating a rhythm of their own as the day began.

> C-130 rollin' down the strip,
> airborne ranger on a one-way trip.
> Stand up, hook up, shuffle to the door,
> jump right out on the count of four.
> If my 'chute don't open wide,
> I got another one by my side.
> And if that 'chute should fail me too,
> look out ground, I'm coming through.

I forget now how far we ran on those first mornings, but by the end of Basic Training we were up to six miles every morning, ending out of breath, our shaved heads slick with sweat, our shirts soaked, all the song run out of us. We gathered once again on the drill pad to stretch and steam and catch our breaths, our voices gone now. The sun had come up sometime while we ran, and gray light filtered over the drill pad, which was always a revelation because we had been running for what seemed forever and thought the night might never end. It was easy in those days to forget where you were and how long you had been there and what you were doing. Easier to put the body on autopilot, to follow only, to respond when called to. Easier to run into the morning singing.

I've learned since then that someone knew that, perhaps Pvt. Willie Duckworth, who created, on one long march through swamps and rough terrain and night, the "Duckworth" chant, which raised the spirits of other soldiers during World War II. Or maybe Baron von Steuben, when he brought close-order drill techniques to Revolutionary War soldiers as a way to perfect timing and to create a greater sense of camaraderie. Or even further back, to Africa and slaves who brought call and response to cotton fields in order to lighten the workload, to make the day pass quicker, to give hope to those without any.

But we knew none of that then, only that here was a way to pass the interminable mornings. And some mornings, the world began exploding as we ran, when artillery was fired in the far distance and the ground trembled beneath us. And some mornings it seemed, as we sang about soldiers on a hill or a C-130 rolling down the strip or what to do in case we die in a combat zone (box us up and ship us home), that we were in a combat zone, which was, I suppose, the point.

Mama, Mama, can't you see,
what the army's done for me?

After first light the song changed.

I should say now that part of what I am calling cadence is only rhythm—our days were planned. Sectioned into smaller parts: run, chow, marching. First class, marching, chow. Marching, second class, marching, third class, marching, chow. More marching. More cadences called through the long white afternoons, and finally, as night came, another run, this one with the heat of the day still on us but the weight of the day gone. We had survived once again, and we ran with night falling, clapping our hands, happy with our place in the world, at least for this moment. After the run we would wash our clothing and write letters and hopefully receive them. We would lie on our bunks and feel the exhaustion of a day's work and still hear the songs thrumming through our heads about the soldier on the hill, about the early morning rain. About Mama and what the army had done for us.

But we're not there yet. When first light fell and our run ended, we double-timed back to the barracks to wipe our bodies with towels—no time for a shower—and dress. After the run, the aches and pains were gone but for a stitch in our sides that would fade on its own. The blood was pumping and adrenaline flowing and there was only this day to get through, only this day to worry about. Whatever cadence we had called was still in our heads—a C-130, an airborne ranger, an unnamed enemy—so that any worries seemed unimportant, any aches easily forgotten.

From the barracks we ran back to the drill pad, then marched to chow. Our cadences here took on a different tone, one I've tried to figure out since the years I left the army and have watched the world explode in war, most of those explosions from bombs of our making, our missiles and men always in the forefront, our technology always ready to shock and awe. If our morning runs needed some motivation, our marches in the daylight must have needed to teach some lesson. We knew we were being broken down and then built back up in the army way, but it only occurred to me years later that the songs might have had something to do with that as well. That songs stick in the head and filter down to the heart. That rhythm moves on its own, and the words can become lodged like a bullet in the brain.

We marched to chow calling cadence through the open corridors. In the mess hall, even our eating took on a rhythm. We shuffled down the line, speaking only to point out what food we wanted, then ate in silence. We had four minutes to finish, and then we were out again, marching toward our first class of the day, where we would learn to treat sucking chest wounds or what to do in case of a nuclear, biological, or chemical attack, and it seems logical now that our cadences took on a different tone.

> Gonna kill some dirty commies,
> turn around and burn their mommies,
> stab their babies in the back,
> put 'em on a roast and rack,
> Place 'em in a barbecue,
> it makes them very soft to chew,
> pick 'em clean down to the bone,
> and back to the jungle I will roam.

We called this cadence on the way to the rifle range or the grenade course or hand-to-hand training. To the bayonet course or the pugil-stick ring. Any time we held a weapon in our hands, any time we were about to simulate killing.

We loved this cadence, called by a drill sergeant named Kuykendall, whose big booming voice made us think he really wanted to kill commies, that he missed roaming the jungle in search of them. Sergeant Adams carried seventy-five pounds of extra weight in his rucksack when we went on long marches, because, he said, if war ever came, he would not fall behind—he was conditioning himself for battle. Drill Sergeant Camacho had arms the size of missiles. Jackson was a Golden Gloves boxer. First Sergeant Pemberton's favorite phrase was "fuck 'em and feed 'em fish heads," and we thought all the drill sergeants were only biding their time until another war broke out and they could be released from garrison duty and go kill something.

This might be a good time to mention that when we fired our M16s we imagined commies and burning and eating their children. Kuykendall's "commie" cadence must have been a holdover from Vietnam, because by my time in the military, the Cold War had ended and the Berlin Wall had fallen, but we did not yet (soon, very soon, I promise) have another enemy to hate in the world, so we called this cadence, which, I must repeat, I loved. I say this first to hold to truthfulness and second so that I will not be able to absolve myself, to set myself apart from the other soldiers I served with or give myself special treatment. I loved it. We all did. We thought it funny. We sang louder when this one came—about killing commies, about stabbing mommies. Burning babies. Barbecuing them. We were eighteen and had never heard of the My Lai massacre or the siege of Stalingrad. We might have read *Slaughterhouse-Five* but didn't know about the firebombing of Dresden. Or Nagasaki or Hiroshima except in the distant way of history books. We hadn't seen that little girl running down the road with napalm on her skin. But this is what I want you to know, because this is important—we fucking loved it.

> Don't bludgeon a seal
> just to make a meal,
> do it 'cause you want to hear
> that little fucker squeal,
> and stomp them in the head
> until you get your kicks,
> then poke them in the eye with
> your eye-pokin' sticks.

We sang this one in the mornings as well. Before first light and after night fell were the times for emotional cadences, full of heartache and loneliness, that soldier on the hill again. But mornings were for killing. "We kill more before nine a.m. than most people do all day," the drill sergeants said, and we sent up a cheer. Remember now, we've only been here a few weeks. Our morale is still shaky. We still miss our mothers, our girl-friends. We cry at night and everyone ignores it. For those who enlisted for six years, there's no going home, not for a long, long time, and the days seem even longer.

So mornings are for killing cadences, dirty commies and baby seals and yellow birds on the windowsill. We loved the seal cadence even more than eating babies. Because although there's a rhyme, there's no reason. Or rather there is a reason—there's joy in killing. Delight in destruction, pleasure in caus-ing pain. We don't kill for any honest reasons—not to feed or clothe ourselves—but to satisfy the craving for killing inside all of us.

So the song says. *Do it 'cause you want to hear that little fucker squeal.* And who can deny there is a fascination with death in-side us, at seventeen or eighteen, carrying an M16 on the way to the rifle range, artillery exploding in the distance, low rumbles like distant thunder, the earth shaking in response? We packed inside of what were called cattle cars, all of us standing like cattle, and perhaps there were those among us who thought we might be headed for the slaughterhouse, but instead of think-ing, we sang of baby seals and stomping and bludgeoning and eye poking them.

At the rifle range we fell out of the cattle cars and into forma-tion, where we were told to keep our rifles pointed downrange and always on safety, but we were thinking of killing. We fell out of formation and lay prone on the shaking earth and zeroed our rifles in, some of us drawing baby seals and baby communists on our zero targets and trying to put their eyes out, some of us calling our M16s "eye-poking sticks" because they seemed so. We sat in the ungodly heat and slipped cartridges into our clips, and after we had zeroed our weapons in, we went to the line and opened them up on rock and roll, another cadence here, this one of three-round bursts, of the bullhorned drill sergeant's voice asking if there is anyone downrange is there anyone downrange is there anyone downrange. In the heat, the distant targets shimmered and the rifle reports echoed to the far hills and back, and inside our heads was the song of it all, the cadence of these hot days.

> Ain't no need in calling home,
> Jody's on your telephone.
> Ain't no need in going home,
> Jody's got your girl and gone.

Jody is a recurring character in army cadences, a lazy shiftless bum but one who has the power to attract females formerly attracted to us. Absence, it seems, does not make the heart grow fonder, at least according to our cadence calls, and Jody, in verse, took over everything we once had. While we were learning to be soldiers, Jody was sleeping with our girlfriends. He was driving our cars, eating our food, using our telephones—all the things we didn't get to do. He lived a luxurious lifestyle, one we no longer had. He took over our houses for himself, threw our clothes out the window, and we believed this could happen because we had left our homes and had our clothes taken away and did not know when we would see our girlfriends.

Jody in cadence became an instrument, a tool to shape men into soldiers. He served to detach soldiers from homelife and all the things they could no longer have. He was a mark at which to aim aggression. When mail time rolled around every night, someone—Buist or Talley or Sykes—got a letter from home and learned his girlfriend had left him, his fiancée had called off the marriage, his wife had slept with another man.

"I'll kill that motherfucker," Sykes, who was from the South Side of Chicago, said, and sometimes on the rifle range you could see in a man's eyes the need to kill. The anger and aggression, the hurt that comes out as hate. Then the disconnect, for after a few days Sykes or Talley or Buist would say he didn't need that fucking bitch anyway, and we'd all agree he was better off without a woman who slept around on him, which was another thing the Jody cadences taught us, that women were never to be trusted, for they had no control over themselves and were often swept away by someone as sorry as Jody.

Jody then served as a symbol of civilian life. The world will take your girlfriend, your wife, your house, your car, your respect. But here, in the army, none of those things will happen. The army is your wife, your lover. The army will feed and clothe you, will give you shelter. What else, the idea is, do you need?

My girl's a vegetable,
she's in the hospital.
And I would do anything
to keep her alive.
She's got no arms or legs,
that's why I call her Peg,
but I would do anything
to keep her alive.
She's got a new TV,
it's called an EKG,
and I would do anything
to keep her alive.
One night I played a joke,
pulled the plug and watched her choke,
but I would do anything
to keep her alive.

There was another version of this cadence titled "My Girl's a Chorus Girl," a Chicago girl, and the narrator would buy anything to keep her in style, the unspoken argument here that the girl is a prostitute, but we liked the vegetable version best. Like the clubbing of baby seals or eating of barbecued children, we found it funny. I would say we didn't take it seriously, but there must have been something in our dark hearts it spoke to, some suggestion of the tragedy we might have been looking for.

Despite the narrator's repeated claim that he loves this girl and would do anything to keep her alive, he makes fun of her plight. He calls her names. He makes fun of her life-support system (he is, obviously, not her life-support system). He plays a joke by watching her die a little. As if she is an embarrassment or a thing that holds little value.

This one was only ever called by the male drill sergeants when the female commander wasn't around. Which brings up several questions about its intention, about women in the military and how they are viewed, about how men are supposed to view them. As a motivational tool then, quadriplegic girlfriends rank evenly with the burning of communist babies or the bludgeoning of baby seals—a joke, a thing to lift morale.

The drill sergeants knew that, of course, every night those letters came in, Sykes's girlfriend leaving him, Billings's wife asking for a divorce. After a long time as military trainers, the drill sergeants knew how men serving longed for the women they had left behind, so they attempted to deconstruct them into parts: a prostitute for sale, a woman with no arms or legs or hair, just patches of it here and there.

See the soldier on the hill,
he is not afraid to kill.
See the soldier on the hi-i-i-ill
in the early morning rain.
See the soldier in the sky,
he is not afraid to die.
See the soldier in the sky-y-y-y
in the early morning rain.

In the evenings we came back to this one again. We sang it so often the refrain echoed in our heads. It's a sad, slow song. We could hear the rain falling in the drill sergeant's trembling voice. As if this had happened, was happening, would happen. As if there were always a soldier on a hill and always would be.

We sang this one in the morning and the evening. At the beginning and end of day, as if all our days should end thinking of the soldier. Our days were long and hot and lonely, full of despair, but this soldier on the hill, the one who is not afraid to kill, the one who is not afraid to die, has sacrificed everything, and here we only have a few rough days to get through. That is the lesson of this song—when a man wearing the same uniform as you has given everything, you have no right to complain about a run or a few push-ups. Or being tired. Or hungry. Or hot or cold or afraid.

We were often all these things. And marching back from the rifle range, sweat soaked and streaked with dirt, burning in our boots, we sang of the soldier. After a sudden storm soaked us through and our clothes clung sodden to our wet cold skin, we thought of the soldier on the hill. Through long nights with fake artillery flashes going off overhead and real ones in the distance, we hummed to keep ourselves awake, and our humming was always of this make-believe soldier, this creation of cadence that rattled around in our heads.

The soldier dies in the end, of course. This is what soldiers do. While laying here to rest, he caught a bullet in the chest. But he wants his wife not to cry, in the early morning rain.

A yellow bird
with a yellow bill
was perched upon
my windowsill.
I lured him in
with crumbs of bread,
and then I smashed
his little head.

Cadences fall into one of a few categories. The soldier on the hill in the early morning rain is meant to motivate, a romantic image of death in a foreign country. There is no defined enemy, only the image: the tireless soldier who has yet grown tired but still stands in the cold rain, who left his wife and left his child, who went off to fight a war, and there is in these words a sense of pride, of selflessness, a sacrifice for some undefined greater good. He will be mourned but also idolized. He is a symbol of a soldier. Freedom, as we will learn, is never mentioned.

Another category is what I'll call madness. Jody sleeping with a soldier's wife or girlfriend instills anger. Clubbing baby seals or eating communist children incites aggression, a gleeful delight in killing, in reducing death down to a humorous cadence. A soldier who would barbecue babies is a soldier so caught up in the war he has become mad, but there's the lingering idea in the lyrics that war can become something he loves, the enemy a thing he hates so much that he loses all sense of rightfulness, but in doing his job of killing the enemy, whatever he chooses to do is rightful.

All cadences are designed to help morale. A soldier may laugh at Jody's antics but they also prepare him for what may one day happen (almost half of all military marriages end in less than ten years). The girl lying in the hospital hooked to her new TV (it's called an EKG) reduces women to a burden a soldier must bear, and the idea in this one is that women are not worth the trouble they cause. Pulling the plug to watch her choke is an ominous foreshadowing of what a soldier might finally do to rid himself of whatever keeps him from serving the army. The "othering" of groups—women, communists, baby seals—draws men closer together. Us versus them. Good versus evil. You're either for us or against us, and if you aren't for us, you must be against us.

One word we never heard in any cadence is freedom. We sang often of death and killing and communism, of the ideal soldier standing in the rain or jumping from a plane, but never freedom. Or democracy or right or righteousness. Not a force of good in the world. Not peacekeeping or peacekeepers or bringing peace. Soldiers know what their job is, and it has nothing to do with peace.

To soldiers, these are abstract concepts. Freedom is a weekend pass. It's going home, getting out of the army for a few days or a few weeks or forever. Freedom is sleeping past four a.m.

It's seeing a girlfriend, a mother, a father, a brother, a wife. Freedom has nothing to do with foreign countries. There is no freedom in war, just more of the same thing the soldier experiences every day: long hours of waiting, endless drills, bad food, boredom, preparation for what may never occur but must be prepared for anyway, only now the threat of death is thrown in as well. Bombs may fall from the sky. Missiles streak in through the clouds. Landmines are stepped on, LEDs hit, snipers striking from the blue hills all around.

"Freedom" is a word politicians and civilians use, not soldiers.

Here we go again,
same old shit again.
Marching down the avenue,
I don't know when we'll be through,
but I'll be glad and so will you.

But we sang of death often, for death is a common recurrence in cadences. I suppose now these cadences were in some ways meditations upon death, glorifications of dying in war, preparations for it. Or, in some of the others, preparations to kill. To create unthinking men, unafraid to stab babies in the back, put 'em on a roast and rack. To see women as jokes, to pull a plug and watch them choke. In war, every kill means a death, and by preparing for one, we must have been preparing for the other.

We didn't know that then. On August 2, we would return from a run, singing of soldiers on the hill and C-130s rolling down the strip, to learn that Saddam Hussein had invaded Kuwait, and we stood in silence on the drill pad as our leaders announced that it looked as if we were going to war. The United Nations passed Resolution 660, condemning the invasion and demanding the immediate withdrawal of Iraqi troops. They did not need to tell us what would happen if Iraq did not withdraw.

In the next few days the 101st and 82nd Airborne Divisions were mobilized. The aircraft carriers *Eisenhower* and *Independence* slipped through the Suez Canal. The first F-15s arrived from Langley, and each morning, before we ran singing of soldiers dying in foreign countries, we came down to see the news from the Gulf written on a chalkboard, the mobilization of forces, the resolutions and sanctions passed by the UN.

Then we ran, farther and faster than we had before. I want to say our voices were louder. Many of us would go home after training and never see the Gulf, never stand on a hill or jump from the sky, but we went through our last days singing, adhering to the old rhythms, the old songs. We ran in the mornings and evenings. We marched to class with our young voices echoing off the walls of the barracks all around us. And when we returned to the barracks late at night, we lay dreaming not of home but of war.

Our last night in Basic Training, our parents had flown in or driven through the night to see us. They were waiting on the drill pad as we came back from wherever we had been, and the drill sergeants marched us in place for what seemed forever, our voices louder and louder and louder, echoing off the buildings all around. The drill sergeants wanted our parents to see us and hear us, to feel our voices ringing out into the summer night. Caught up in the cadence, the sheer joy of singing, whether about dirty commies or women lying dead in hospital beds, whether about soldiers dying in the early morning rain or soldiers falling from the sky, we didn't know that we were only marching in place.

Which is to say we never knew where we were going and would only realize later that we never went anywhere. We woke every morning to reveille and dressed with the dark outside the windows, then ran down to the drill pad and all over the base, past the old World War II cannons and the fighter jets, past the tanks and helicopters and bronze statues of men long dead, everything dark, lit only in pools of yellow light that threw our shadows out large beside us. We might have been circling forever, as if we had always been here and always would be. We might have been lost in the darkness. We might have been on any base, wearing any uniform in the world, blindly following the men chosen to lead us, who could have taken us anywhere.

ONE BOOT,
NO PANTS

Someone wore the wrong sock so we were sent upstairs to change.

We all had to wear the same uniform, and the wrong boot or blouse could throw the entire army into disarray, it seemed. The idea here was not uniform so much as uniformity, all men moving as one, but we didn't know that then, concerned as we were with our own thin skins. It hadn't yet occurred to us that the drill sergeants could always find some reason to force us into physical exercise until sweat streamed into our shoes. An untucked blouse or boot string meant an extra mile run, and a dropped machine gun made us want to murder the man who did it for the punishment that would be visited upon us. Pain was to make us pay attention to every tiny detail, every called command. Inattention in training got a soldier in trouble, the drill sergeants said, but inattention anywhere else got him dead. I would offer now that mismatched socks do not lose wars, but at eighteen, just out of high school, barely shaving, and scared all the time, I believed what the drill sergeants were saying: about socks and shoes, about boots and blouses.

Outside, it was 170 degrees or somewhere close. In the barracks, our voices rebounded off the tile floors. We were given explicit orders what to wear, so we stood at our lockers looking for one green sock and one white one, one black glove and one green, one winter bottom and one summer top, one combat boot and one dress shoe. If we couldn't stay in simple uniform, one of the drill sergeants was bellowing, he'd give us a new uniform to wear, one that wasn't so simple.

"You'll learn to follow fucking orders," he said.

When we assembled downstairs in our new outfits, the drill sergeants went up and down the row inspecting us. Diamond had the white sock on the wrong foot and we were punished with push-ups. Hoteling had on summer bottoms with a winter top and we did sit-ups so long I thought my stomach might seize up. Ebel had no gloves. Perez had forgotten his belt.

After an hour of exercise in the exhausting heat, we were sent back upstairs to search for our shower shoes. We needed PT shorts now, a brown T-shirt, a soft cap and rucksack and only one dog tag, and when we came back down in our motley gear, already as tired as the days were long, we were punished again because Benavidez wore a white T-shirt instead of brown and Buist brought boots instead of shower shoes.

When the drill sergeants saw Ramirez's fucked-up rucksack, we were sent back up, all of them shouting that we would, by God America, learn to follow commands unquestioningly, to become goddamn fucking soldiers. Now we needed our Kevlar helmets and running shoes, brown boxers, white T-shirt, pants with the legs on our arms, underwear on our heads or something just as stupid, though I'll say underwear on our heads because it's close to heads up our asses. Later it would occur to me that this was an endless exercise, like rolling a stone uphill or trying to sweep all the sand out of the Middle East so we might pave it with parking lots. That we would keep repeating the same futile efforts until the end of the world. We never seem to see what is coming for us: not the forest for the trees, not the war swimming out of the sudden future, not our hands right in front of our faces because of the underwear covering them.

When Alarid wore briefs instead of boxers, we were sent back up to change once more. The next uniform was even worse. I don't remember what it was, what combination of clothing the drill sergeants cooked up, except to say that it was hot, and I was tired, and I didn't know what I was doing any more. Not in training, not in the army. The drill sergeants stalked the halls shouting an endless diatribe about our failures, a demand that we rise above our worthless beginnings to become something greater, though I'll say now that shower shoes won't teach us a lesson about our human frailties unless it's that we'll keep doing the same thing again and again while hoping for a different result. Then, there was no time to question, no time to do anything other than what we were told. I was standing with one boot on, no pants, my underwear rolled in my hand and sweat tracking down my face, not yet old enough to understand the world around me. I'd like to create some convenient metaphor here about how the uniforms we wear change us or about how often we are exposed to inhumanities and fail to fight back, but I don't think anyone would listen to a man in mismatched socks. Let's just say we ran up and down the stairs a dozen times, until we didn't know any longer what we were doing. That we only listened to the commands called to us because we had no other choice. That we acted accordingly. That men in uniforms all over the world, no matter what color or combination of clothing, are only doing what they are commanded by men with more power. No matter how silly it may seem. No matter how naked they are in the end.

IS THERE ANYONE DOWNRANGE?

On the rifle range the heat hit hard, got up under your helmet and into your head. The sun at Fort Sill stood overhead like something we wanted to forget, and the horizon lay hazed with the awful heat. Later that night, lightning would run from cloud to cloud in the western sky as if a war had arrived, and later that summer a war would arrive, but that day we were only worried about the heat, how it got inside you and stole all your strength. We were worried whether we could hit enough targets with our M16s to qualify as marksmen but not yet worried about what it might mean when we succeeded.

"Is there anyone downrange, is there anyone downrange, is there anyone downrange?" the range NCO said through his bullhorn, his voice echoing to the far hills and back. "If so, let yourself be known by sight or sound."

He paused, perhaps waiting for a shout or a sign that some-one was indeed downrange and in danger of being shot, and when no one declared himself, he allowed us to open fire. For days we'd been learning to shoot: to breathe properly while aiming, to squeeze the trigger slowly. We put dimes on the barrels of our rifles to teach steadiness. We trained our lungs to stillness. We lay in the dirt with one eye closed and peered through the sights and pulled the trigger. We watched the dust kick up downrange.

In two days we would go to another range where targets would pop up out of the Oklahoma dirt. A day after that it would be bayonets we learned to wield, and after that grenades and claymores and M60s. Somewhere in there we'd learn how to splinter a crushed leg, how to administer for nerve gas. We'd learn to call in air strikes, to use gas masks and MOPP gear, to navigate through forest or field.

Now we were prone in the dirt, sweating and hoping we hit our targets so we could get out of the heat. When it came my turn, I closed one eye and squeezed the trigger, my M16 making my ears ring. Sweat ran in my eyes, but I had grown up shooting guns. My grouping was tight as virgin pussy, Drill Sergeant White told me, so I was sent downrange with Talley and Ellenberger and others who had qualified. We walked amid the burnt grass and brass casings under the big white sun, all of us looking back ready to yell if the range NCO raised his bullhorn.

At the far end of the range a bunker had been built into the hill, and when we reached the bunker we were put on target detail. After each round of firing we had to lower and replace the targets through holes cut into the hillside. The bunker was three feet of concrete under five feet of earth, but often the bullets would enter the bunker through the target holes and ricochet around. Because of this we wore bulletproof vests. All around us the air filled with metal, the sound like someone shooting street signs. We stood as far back inside the bunker as we could, hiding inside our helmets, hoping the bullets wouldn't find us. Talley said "fuck" three or four times. Ellenberger said "assholes" over and over.

Every few minutes the shooting stopped and the all clear sounded and we climbed out of our holes to change the targets. Someone swept up the stray bullets, shaking, then we covered ourselves again as the range NCO asked if anyone was downrange, if anyone was downrange, if anyone was downrange, his bullhorned voice barely audible through the thick earth.

We spent the rest of that day and most of a week in the concrete bunker with the bullets ricocheting around us while the rest of our men learned to kill. Some days we stayed so late the sun began to set and the bunker grew dark. In the last light, the horizon lay limned with fire, as if the missiles had finally flown and this were the twilight hour of humanity, so we named the bunker End of the World.

"It's lonely here at End of the World," Talley said, eating an MRE, "and the food sucks."

"There are no women at End of the World," Ellenberger told us. "Only men and the sound of metal."

When the war started in the winter, I would imagine myself in that bunker again, as Iraqi soldiers crawled out of the earth and surrendered to army troops advancing in a long line across the desert. The oil fires burning on the horizon seemed to mark some shift in what made sense, and I'd see the bullets bouncing around the bunker, the closest I've ever been to being shot. We were all of us boys in men's boots, worried for what the days in front of us would look like. We didn't know when we'd be asked to raise our rifles. We didn't know when the bullets would bounce around us.

"Is there anyone downrange?" the man with mirrored glasses said, and there in the bunker amid the ricocheting bullets, we yelled, "Yes," laughing because we hadn't yet realized we could cry. "We're downrange," we said. "For the love of God, don't shoot." But they always did, and there was nothing we could say to stop them.

COLORS

— — — — — — — — — — — —

Drill Sergeant White was black and Drill Sergeant Black was white. Private Blue was white and Private Brown was black, and Green was closer to yellow, but we all turned gray when word came down we were going to war.

Our parents went white with worry. We blanked our faces with black. Our drill sergeants said we were all brothers in the army, green as the uniforms we wore over our different skins. "I only see green," said Drill Sergeant White, but after the news of war came down we needed to other the color of the men we might fight, so we sang slurs about sand and camel jockeys until we went red with laughter.

When the war began, our TVs turned to fire. We watched gray bodies dug from the brown dirt. And when it was over we held our hands to our hearts while the flag waved like a symbol, like the pictures we drew as children of a white house, red sun, the big blue sky of the future.

WESTERN CIV

My first college class was in a lecture hall with chairs bolted to the concrete floor. The room reminded me of a movie theater—the floor was sticky, as if it had endured decades of spilled soft drinks and popcorn butter, and the seats rose in tiers toward the back. The last few rows smelled of urine and body odor. The chalkboard looked like a dead screen.

The class was 8 a.m. Western Civilization, and most of the students were asleep. They stunk of alcohol and pot from the night before, their bodies on some sort of college autopilot that allowed them to be physically present but mentally checked out. Girls wore their pajamas and bunny slippers, their hair piled atop their heads, twisted into something that managed to be both elaborate and unkempt at the same time. Some of them brought pillows and curled up in their chairs.

Dr. Kruegar came in at 8 a.m. sharp, his lecture beginning as soon as he entered, before he even set down the briefcase containing the notes he never used. He lectured for fifty minutes, chalking the long board in sections, then going back to the far left to erase and start again. When the bell rang, he stopped lecturing, told us we'd start next time where we left off, and we dispersed toward the rest of the day, back to our dorms for another few minutes of unconsciousness or to the cafeteria for a bowl of Count Chocula cereal. The next class, he would walk in at eight, say, "We stopped last time at the reign of Amenhotep" or "When the bell rang last class, the pyramids were just being built," and start again.

This was late summer 1990, just weeks after Saddam Hussein invaded Kuwait. A few days before starting college I had been in Basic Training, sleeping in the rain under a poncho thrown over a bush. My brother had enrolled me in college while I was going through the gas chamber or rappelling from the side of a cliff. I moved into my dorm room late the evening before classes started, but I was still used to military life, not yet ready for college. Because my head was still shaved, I sat in the far back corner, where we used to sit in movie theaters if we wanted to make out with our girlfriends, but I just wanted to be left alone. I didn't trust myself to speak to people, afraid a military word or cadence would slip out. Sometimes, when I walked to class, I heard myself chanting under my breath, rhythms of cadence and call instilled in me on hot mornings before first light and evening runs as the sun was going down. I woke often in the middle of the night, wondering where I was, how long before the drill sergeants came screaming in or tossed a smoke bomb through the door. Every evening, after classes, I went down to the common room to catch the news on TV about the impending war, and every morning before Western Civ I walked to the communications building to get the newspaper. On weekends I stayed up too late and drank too much, sitting alone in a dark room with the blue glow of the TV etched across my face, but I managed, for the first few weeks anyway, to make my classes.

The Western Civ classroom was less than half-full most days. It would seat two hundred, I guessed, and there were maybe a hundred and fifty students the first day, but the numbers slowly began to decline when people decided sleeping an extra hour was more important than the beginnings of modern civilization, as if sleep were a rare commodity denied the young, unlike education, which was so abundant you could afford opportunities to let it pass. Only one person sat near me in the back row, a girl with dirty-blond hair and black roots who wore too much eye shadow. She smelled like cigarette smoke, and her T-shirts often had some message on them like *Co-ed Naked Softball* or *I Need A %^*$ing Vacation!* She sat at the end of the row on the first day, and I could see her watching me when she thought I wasn't looking. The next day she had moved a seat closer, and another seat the day after that.

By the end of the second week she sat next to me, the two of us in the far back corner by ourselves. There were maybe fifty students in the class, most of them scattered in the middle rows, either listlessly taking notes or open-mouthed sleeping. She told me her name was Heather and she thought military men were sexy. This was delivered—with no trace of self-consciousness or embarrassment—within the first five minutes of our first conversation. She rubbed my head, where the stubble from my last buzz cut was just long enough to be soft. She let her hand trail down my arm. She was a few years older than me, twenty-two or twenty-three, the kind of student who has dropped out of college once or twice already and is giving it a final shot before settling into whatever line of work she has been doing since high school, getting married and having children, trying to quit smoking every few years.

After informing me that military men were sexy, she asked when I was going to Iraq. I knew I would not be going, but no matter what I said, I couldn't disabuse her of the notion. At other times, trying to impress girls at parties or guys bigger than me, I'd say I was waiting to hear about my deployment any day now, and the looks of respect they gave me made the lie worth it, but when I told Heather I wasn't going to war, she didn't believe me. She would ask if I had been activated, I would say no, and then she would ask how long I thought the flight to Iraq was. Or she'd ask if I thought it would be hot over there, I'd tell her I had no idea, and she'd ask if I had to get any shots, like for malaria or typhoid fever.

"I've heard you have to get shots to go to some countries," she told me one day, the phrase "some countries" meaning "anywhere not in the contiguous forty-eight." It was like she had selective hearing, the way Dr. Kruegar would announce for weeks that we had a test coming up, and still we would all look bewildered when he began to pass out the exams. "A test?" some guy fresh from a power nap would say drowsily, drool running down his chin. "When did this happen, because I certainly didn't know about it," even though he would have the word TEST and the date written in big block letters across a page of his notebook, just above the doodles of werewolves or kittens he had drawn before passing out.

"You might die," Heather said one day. Her fingernails were painted purple. "Doesn't that scare you?"

I told her I was pretty sure I was safe, that all the troops being shipped to the Middle East had already been shipped. I didn't know if that was true, but I hoped it would stop her from asking questions I had no idea how to answer. When we first heard news of the war in Basic, we pretended we wanted to go, but that night after lights out the silence spread through the barracks like smoke.

"I would be sad if you had to go," she wrote in her notebook one day while Dr. Kruegar lectured, her purple pen carving out big looping letters, then angled it so I could see. After a minute she bent down to write again: "Even sadder if something happened to you."

When I wrote "I would be pretty sad myself," she slapped my arm as if I had offended her somehow. I supposed I wasn't taking her vision of my deployment and subsequent death seriously enough, but in my defense, we were halfway around the world, in a classroom with sticky floors, half of the class asleep, the rest hardly listening to lectures on how the pyramids were constructed and how the ancient Egyptians thought the pharaohs were gods, that there existed another world after this one.

We seemed to exist in another world as well, one in which we ignored everything not directly related to our own small skins. Heather's view of the war was a movie version of leaving and returning, a departure and arrival at an airport gate. The guy down the hall from me said we should nuke the Middle East and be done with it, a sentiment I heard often that year before the bombs began to fall on Baghdad. I wasn't sure what my view was. Most mornings I woke way too early. I'd hear the ROTC running past my dorm, calling cadence, and think I should be there with them. Or I'd just wake at 4 a.m., when we had been forced to get up at Basic, my body telling me it was time to rise and fucking shine, and on these mornings, after I'd figured out where I was, I'd lie there in the dark and breathe, wondering what I was doing here, what we were all doing. The cafeteria would be empty when I stumbled there at 6 a.m. for a child-sized box of Honey Nut Cheerios, and by eight I'd be just as sleepy as the other students. Sometimes I'd nod off, my chin falling to my chest, then snap awake with that sense of falling you sometimes get, and each time this happened I'd wake to see Heather watching me.

"Do you think you'll get to call or write letters when you're over there?" she would say. "Will you write me?"

During the third week she asked me if I wanted to study together, her look telling me that her version of studying would involve one or both of us losing our clothing while she asked me what I thought being shot would feel like. When I told her my girlfriend wouldn't like that very much, she said, "I won't tell if you won't," and laughed in the way that means "I am joking but I am also very much not joking." I laughed in the way that means "You don't know if I am taking this seriously or not," but I might as well have been waving those cylindrical flashlights the ground crews use at airports—this way to the terminal. She took my hand and wrote her phone number on my palm, with her name and a smiley face and "Call me" below the face.

When I didn't call, I guess she decided the subtle approach wasn't getting anywhere. She came in late the next class, a wreath of smoke circling her, and sat down beside me without looking my way. I thought I was getting the silent treatment, but halfway through class I felt her hand on my knee. She leaned close—I could smell her cigarette breath—and said, "Want me to jerk you off?"

There was hunger in the look she gave me, a longing for physical contact. I recognized it from seeing my own face in the mirror all through high school, after the frantic gropings on buses coming back from football games, the quick feels copped on couches in the light of the TV while fathers wandered around upstairs, occasionally stomping on the floor to let you know they hadn't gone to bed yet, the goodnight kisses on front porches or sitting in idling cars while the curtains were peeled back by suspecting parents. I had met my future wife just before I left for Basic and waited every evening during mail call for her letters, reading and rereading the promises they contained, or I imagined they contained. I knew about wanting the touch and comfort of another human being, although I never thought of such things sitting in a dank classroom learning about the beginnings of civilization. Slave labor and mummies have never turned me on, but there was a war I might be called to and the class was boring, so I guess Heather figured why not, and the way she looked made me think of her sitting alone late at night watching snow fall on the apartment buildings near campus, hoping the phone would ring or someone would stop by.

This is only to say I had no idea how to answer. I had the feeling this was one of those subjects on which she might develop selective hearing, like she had when I told her I wasn't going to die in a war. But to say "not here" had its own problems, as such an answer would imply there was some other place we might go. To mention my girlfriend again would draw the same response as telling her I wasn't going to be shot at any time soon—I might as well be lecturing to a class full of sleeping students.

So while Dr. Kruegar went on about Amenhotep the Magnificent, the Egyptian pharaoh, her fingers wandered—itsy-bitsy spider–like—up my thigh. Her hand was warm and moist. Her mouth hung open slightly. She didn't look at me.

Years later, I'd tell friends this story after a few drinks, and, always, they'd ask what happened, as if that were the most important part. I never answered, preferring an ambiguous ending to voicing what was at best an awkward moment and at worst a defining one. I have found since that it's hard to offer comfort to someone when you don't know what comfort is, when you wake three or four times a night and wonder where you are and why you aren't somewhere else. And it's harder still when said comfort comes in the form of sexual acts in public.

My friends never cared about the classroom or the sticky floor. The way students would slouch down until their necks rested on the seat or curl up with a pillow, how sometimes half the room would be asleep, as if the history of where we came from was less important than closing their eyes for just a moment. How after I got back to my dorm room in the evening I'd find someone to drive me to the liquor store and then sit in my empty room and watch the coverage of the war we all knew was coming. How we all embrace selective hearing and thinking, ignoring signs and signals, believing whatever we want to believe, whatever makes it easier for us to get through the day: that the war doesn't affect us, that we are more attractive than we really are, that we only want to go back to sleep or hide in our own little corner of the classroom. That we aren't lonely and heartbroken and sick at times. I maintain that these are the most important elements, not whether any acts were completed or not completed, if flesh was touched or not touched, but no one ever agreed with me. They needed to *know*.

The rest then, is this:

Heather disappeared from class not long after midterms, and I never saw her again. Over a quarter of the class dropped out before December, before the United Nations passed Resolution

678, setting a deadline for Iraq to withdraw from Kuwait or face military action. I guess their grades were sloping downward and they realized they had no chance of passing the final. I'd see them in the hallway, hair gone awry and faces creased from sleep, and wonder what they were doing. The next semester, when all our TV screens bloomed from the bombs in CNN's night-vision cameras, I'd wonder what any of us were doing walking the halls half-asleep, no interest in the courses we were taking, drawn on weekends to dark rooms and loud music and too much alcohol, wandering alone through the shifting bodies searching for something we couldn't quite define, all of us with the world in our hands and not able to hold on to the smallest piece of it.

At the end of the semester I would be put on academic probation, and at the end of the year I would be kicked out of school. When the war started during my second semester, I skipped every class—every single one—to watch those night-vision cameras, the endless air sorties, the falling bombs and antiaircraft fire rising up like signs of the coming apocalypse, the missiles falling on Tel Aviv, and finally, in the heart of February, just a few days after my nineteenth birthday, the tanks and APCs and multiple launch rocket systems rolling across the desert toward Baghdad and the end. By the time it was over, I had missed too many classes to make up, so I stayed in my dorm room and waited for the next part of my life to begin. The next summer, as the troops were returning home, I was in Fort Jackson, South Carolina, and every person we saw outside the base thought we had just come from Desert Storm, mistaking us for returning soldiers, for something we were not.

Years later, when a new war began right where the last one left off, it occurred to me how often we offer hand jobs instead of the intimacy of attempting to understand. We say "freedom" and "hero" in an effort to find comfort in the actions of soldiers we'd rather not think about beyond the national anthem, the faux patriotism of planes flying over a football field. "Thank you for your service" is a quick release, a way of avoiding any responsibility for actions outside our own. It's comforting ourselves so we can claim we've done something, a hand job to the idea of hero we've formed from an ignorant understanding of war.

But then, I only imagined what would happen if Heather's hand didn't stop its upward climb. What if Dr. Kruegar looked up from his lecture or someone woke long enough to turn around? There I would be—a girl's hand wrapped around me, most of the class asleep, a war beginning not far from where Amenhotep the Magnificent had once ruled, where the pyramids were raised as causeways to heaven and ancient men had accomplished the unbelievable—there I would be, frantically scribbling notes, trying to understand the whole of western civilization.

FLIGHT

In the summer of 1991, along with eleven other men and women around my age—nineteen—I boarded a plane to Charlotte and the second half of my military training. There were three girls in the group who had never flown, and they held each other's hands as the plane taxied down the runway, screaming when the pilot pushed the throttle forward. They hugged each other the entire flight, their lips moving in silent prayer. They screamed when we lifted off and screamed when we hit pockets of turbulence and screamed when the plane banked for its final approach. When we landed in Charlotte they walked unsteadily off the plane, still holding on to one another.

Inside the terminal, the three girls recovered. They laughed about their earlier fear. They were younger than the rest of us, still in high school. They had never been away from home, and though we made fun of them in the way that men will sometimes laugh at what scares them too, we told them there was nothing to be ashamed of, that fear affects everyone differently.

Walking through the Charlotte airport in our uniforms, some people shook our hands, confusing us with soldiers returning from the Middle East. The Gulf War had just ended, and there were soldiers everywhere, celebrations erupting at every terminal, men hugging women hugging children.

I had been scared on the plane too. The summer before, I had flown from Little Rock to Dallas on a small jet, and then from Dallas to Fort Sill on a puddle jumper, a twin prop that was so loud I couldn't understand the pilot's words and so small there was only one attendant, who couldn't hear over the noise of the propellers or yell loud enough when outlining the safety procedures. Like the three girls, I had been scared of what I was getting myself into. I had joined the military because my father and grandfather had served, but bouncing around between the clouds on that small plane, I had begun to reconsider the wisdom of my decision. When Saddam Hussein invaded Kuwait just a few weeks before I graduated Basic Training, I would reconsider again.

But now the Gulf War had ended, the troops were returning home, we were flying to complete our military training, and the celebrations in the airport made us forget the flight. If there was any lingering fear in us then, it had been placed there by the staff sergeant who briefed us on military travel protocol. This was in Little Rock, right before we boarded the plane, before the girls' fears began to get the better of them.

The first rule was we had to stay together and maintain our military bearing at all times. We were representatives of the U.S. military, and we would behave as such.

We were not to swear or insult anyone or act inappropriately in any way.

We were not to use the word "bomb" or "detonate" or "rifle" or "hijack," so for most of the flight a guy named Bryant and I made up words we could use instead of the forbidden ones. Bryant said "balm" and I said "defecate," and together we created "riffle" and "hijinks," which we found hilarious. Later, as we began to descend toward Charlotte, we wondered why we would not be allowed to say the real ones, concluding that in crazy countries, as we called them, balms and hijinks and defecations were serious threats.

Our gate was at the far end of one of the airport wings, and we walked together, occasionally whispering "defecate" or "hijinks" or laughing about the three girls' silly fear of flying.

We were almost at the gate when we saw the man in the turban. A bank of pay phones hung on one wall, and he stood next to them, turned sideways. He wore black silk robes that matched the turban. He carried a staff—not a cane, but a wrist-thick, five-foot-tall staff with some sort of polished stone atop it. One arm covered the lower part of his face, like a vampire in an old film, and he peered over his arm with eyes I can only describe as beady. A suitcase rested at his feet.

A small crowd had gathered around him. A group of three or four soldiers watched him. Airport security stood nearby, walkie-talkies in their hands.

Ten years later, in 2001, I'd turn on the TV just as the second plane crashed into the South Tower on that morning in September. All that day and into the next the footage rolled, again and again, on video and timed cameras, in frames that could be paused, enlarged, and shrunk, rewound and played again, and again, and again. People jumped from the towers, falling in slow motion, and then the towers collapsed, smoke billowing skyward. There were different angles and different qualities of film and different lighting in each one, as if our collective conscious had captured it but we would all remember it differently.

Not quite a year later, in the summer of 2002, I flew to Arkansas to visit my family. My wife and daughters had flown back a few weeks before, so I was on my own, and since I didn't have to pretend to my daughters that I am not afraid of flying, I started thinking about the plane crashing, about September 11, about those three girls from ten years before, about the man in the black silk robes with the suitcase.

I had an aisle seat, and as I bent over to slide my backpack beneath me, I saw a man coming down the aisle. He had a thick black beard and dark skin, and though he was dressed in jeans and a collared shirt, I remembered hearing that the

9/11 hijinksers had shed their desert robes for western clothes when they boarded those four flights. It was early in the flight and I didn't think the move-about-the-cabin light had come on yet. He had one hand behind him, as if he were reaching for something in his back pocket, which I was sure would be a box cutter that he'd use to slit the throats of the flight attendants, then kick open the cockpit door and bank the plane sharply as we rerouted toward the White House.

All this flickered through my mind, and then the guy sidled past. He was not reaching for a box cutter. He did wear a beard, but his dark skin came from tanning in a lighted bed or lying beside a kidney-shaped pool. He would have looked more at home in Pennsylvania or Ohio than Iraq or Afghanistan, some small town with a name like Wrinkle Creek or Deerfield.

"Why is he looking at us like that?" one of the girls whispered on that summer day in 1991, the Gulf War just over, no threats on the horizon that we could see. I thought she was going to cry. The man looked like he hated us, though I could be conflating memory with what I know now, how simple it is to see others as other, to project our own fears onto different skin.

I'd guess now that the man had never been to a western country, that he was confused as to why so many people had crowded around him as if he were a zoo exhibit. I'd say he simply didn't like to fly and was worried about the immediate future, the same way all of us were as we stood there looking at him.

"He looks like he has a riffle hidden in his robes," one of the guys in our group said. "Or a balm in his briefcase."

More security came down the gates; more soldiers joined the crowd.

"He looks like he wants to defecate us all," we said, not understanding how words work, how easy it is to turn toward the terrible.

We were young then, not educated about the world or human nature or how much hate we can hold. None of us could see the awful future or understand how we would react to the singular moments of our lives, the ones we replay in our heads again and again, wondering what they mean, what we can learn from them.

"Balm," we said. "Balm, balm, balm, balm, bomb."

MOVEMENT

A few months ago on the History Channel, I saw that during World War II, motor scooters were dropped from airplanes. That's all the information the program gave, but one can assume the motor scooters weren't dropped as bombs but rather parachuted, and one can further assume they were recovered once they landed and were then driven to some final destination.

As a recovering history major, this story made me want to know where and when and how they were used, but putting those concerns aside, I began to focus on the logistics. First, the scooters—and, one must also assume, the future operators of the scooters—must have been loaded onto a plane in England and then flown to somewhere over France or Belgium, where they were dropped, with their operators, from the belly of a C-47.

Here I want to imagine motor scooters falling gently from the sky and some farmer in a field of bright tulips looking up to see them. I imagine the operators recovering the scooters in midfall, starting the engines a thousand feet above the ground before landing softly, the tires making purchase, the parachutes being cut away, and then they are off to the Battle of the Bulge or the Black Forest or driving through destroyed Dresden. I don't know.

I just see the drivers, hunched over the handlebars. I think they must have worn scarves and leather bomber jackets against the cold (I always imagine the European theater as being cold).

They wore goggles and leather helmets, and a plume of blue exhaust went out behind them as they raced for the front or carried special documents in their sidecars (they have sidecars in my imagination). In the distance, artillery erupted from the earth, airplanes droned overhead, and in bunkers and basements men and women craned their eyes skyward, as if to see what moved above them.

I don't know what happened when they got where they were going, but thinking of the scooters reminds me of my grandfather, who fought in the Battle of the Bulge and spent the first few months after the war ended driving majors and colonels and brigadier generals around the ruins of European cities. He wasn't on a scooter but in a jeep, no roof, only a windshield, and it must have been cold so I imagine the scarves and goggles and heavy coats again. He was twenty-six years old, a newly minted lieutenant who would later rise high enough to be driven around himself, but that hadn't happened yet, and there was only the aftermath of war, jeeps and tanks and motor scooters everywhere, airplanes overhead, the constant rumbling of engines reverberating off what walls still stood. The entire world seemed shell-shocked, he told me. In the countryside, the roads were filled with refugees, men and women with no homes left, wandering from place to place, trying to find some quiet spot to lie down, moving to the side of the road to let the constant convoys pass. No one knew where they were going. The cities had crumbled around them and people wandered the streets in a daze. When I asked my grandfather where he went and what they did when they got there, he told me of meetings in Bastogne and Berlin, but what he remembered most was the movement, their shadows running along beside them through the ruins.

— — — — — — — — — — —

I spent a considerable amount of time during the first Gulf War thinking of movement. This occurred for several reasons, the first being that I was fascinated with the war and the buildup to it, the great general intake of breath we all drew.

The second reason was that I seemed stuck in some sort of stasis. We all did, like the world was waiting to see what happened next. My stepfather's National Guard unit had been activated in September, and by November he was stationed at Fort Sill, Oklahoma, a five-hour drive from our house, preparing to be shipped overseas.

Every weekend throughout that late fall I came home from college and my mother and I made the drive to see him. It seems now it rained each time, gray skies looming before us, the windshield wipers beating out the same song. My mother smoked with her hands on the wheel, and when I drove she used both hands to hold her cigarette, as if she needed the second to help steady her. In the rain, her cigarette smoke slowly being sucked out the window, we went past churches with signboards out front saying God Bless America and Pray for Our Troops, and I wondered, all through that waiting fall, what the war would bring. Like most of America, I wanted a swift and speedy victory. I wanted Iraq wiped off the map, the Middle East turned into a parking lot, for that was the rhetoric we heard from every war hawk in the country.

Back at college in small-town Arkansas, no one seemed to care about the war. My professors never mentioned it. There were no demonstrations on campus, for or against, as if we'd all decided, collectively, to ignore the whole idea. But at night, after we had all driven to the liquor store for booze we weren't old enough to buy, I could hear the TVs going all up and down the dorm hall: the retired generals talking of battle plans, the Middle East experts explaining the instability that could occur if Hussein were toppled, the Christian leaders claiming Armageddon was coming.

When I went to my own National Guard drills, we rarely mentioned the war. Instead, we inventoried our gear. We trained in the field. We went to the rifle range. I suppose our commanders wanted us ready in case the call came, but at any time of day we could find them—the captains and colonels, the majors and master sergeants—hidden away in an office watching CNN: the deployment of troops and the battle carriers massing, the same as I did every night in my dorm room.

On Fridays I skipped classes and drove home. Some days I wondered if I would bother to drive back. There seemed no reason to return. Some mornings I didn't even get out of bed. Some nights I didn't go to sleep. Most days I didn't go to class, just waited to see what was coming for us all.

When my mother and I arrived at Fort Sill, we had to get clearance, and the officer in charge looked at my short hair as if I should be on his side of the fence. Fort Sill was where I had just completed Basic Training only a few months before, and it felt strange to drive through the base seeing soldiers moving in troop formation, to hear the call of drill sergeants, the response of soldiers in training—I wondered if I should be with them.

During the day, while my mother and stepfather stayed in their hotel room, I drove around the base. I visited my old drill sergeant, who told me how many of the guys I was in Basic with had been shipped overseas. One drill sergeant asked me if I was ready to go, another laughed at my civilian clothes, and still another—the only one—asked how my stepfather was standing up, if he was holding on, if my mother was all right. I could hear, in the distant parts of the base, machine-gun fire, and that night I woke in the hotel wondering where I was. I would do this often in the years I served in the military, first at Basic Training, then AIT, then for years following, wake up and wonder at the dreams I had of being a soldier. I still do sometimes. I dream that I've been called back to the service. I dream of those fall months of late 1990, before the war began, the long, rain-filled drives to Fort Sill, the sadness in my mother's face. My stepfather dreamed, too, in the years after he came back. He told me he dreamed of the long flight to Germany, then to Riyadh. He dreamed of the long drive across the desert during the ground war, then the final push toward Baghdad. He said it wouldn't go away, even years later, as if we're always driving toward war, always moving toward a future we can't see.

— — — — — — — — — — —

And not long after the Gulf War ended, I found myself hurtling through the darkness in the back of a Humvee while explosions echoed in the night. This was winter, and cold, and my National Guard unit was performing maneuvers on Fort Chaffee, navigating with night-vision lenses, tracking the Air Guard as they dropped bombs, the earth rumbling, the night lit in brief flashes bright as day.

Mickey drove, but Chief Parker, sitting in the passenger seat, wore the night-vision lenses. No one could see except Chief, a point Mickey repeated every few seconds.

"I can't see a goddamn thing, Chief."

With no headlights there was only darkness flowing before us, occasionally lit by artillery in the distance, the brief flashes carving the landscape out before us, the road wound like a river. Mickey's hands were white on the wheel.

Chief Parker was in his fifties. He'd been in the National Guard for thirty years. He had a slim mustache like Errol Flynn in a Sabatini film and hair just turning silver. Fog formed on the windshield, and occasionally Chief wiped at it with his sleeve. The night-vision lenses made his silhouette alien in the dark.

He said, "A little to the right."

He said, "Curve coming up. To the left. Twenty degrees."

He said, "Careful now."

Mickey steered according to directions from Chief. At first he'd crept along, his instincts telling him he didn't know what lay ahead. But after a while he pushed the gas and we flew down the road, all but Chief blind.

I sat in the back with Skeeter, a skinny kid still with pimples. When Mickey slammed on the brakes or cursed and swung the wheel, Skeeter let out a little yelp only I could hear over the sound of the engine.

Clouds slid across the face of the moon. Earlier, I had lain at the side of the road and felt the rattle and tread of a passing convoy in the earth beneath me, and when it had gone I radioed size and movement and waited in the night with my hands frozen into claws and my breath in the air before me. Now the Humvee had come for me and we flew down the dark road.

"Are we having fun yet?" Chief said.

In the back, Skeeter and I gripped our rifles. We had blacked out the dash because any lights in the night-vision lenses blinded the wearer. Skeeter's eyes were as big and round as the lenses Chief wore. The dark shapes of trees flipped past the window. We slipped off the side of the road and Chief cursed until Mickey eased us back to safety.

Since the Gulf War, we had been fighting mock battles on weekend field exercises, whispering code words about attacking forces, stringing camouflage netting over our Hummers and armored personnel carriers. Now the war was over, but the threat was always there, and though we'd narrowly missed the Gulf, no one thought we'd miss whatever came next. No one doubted there would be something that came next, because there was always something that came next, something that formed as silently as snow clouds or rattled toward you like a convoy on a dirt road. Something was always careening out of the darkness.

This was ten years before two airplanes struck the Twin Towers and another crashed into a field in Pennsylvania. Before the Pentagon was attacked, before the towers dissolved as most of the world watched. Before the first troops were sent to Afghanistan, before another Iraq war began, where, this time, the speeding armies would not stop sixty miles from Baghdad. It was before Osama bin Laden was shot and killed by SEAL Team Six, before the wars dragged on and on, before the drones multiplied, before cities fell into ruins from the force of bombs and the shadows of soldiers riding through ran long beside them. Before Syria came apart and Benghazi was attacked and Iran was sanctioned and North Korea fired missiles into the sea.

In the distance, artillery rounds fell and fighters flew in low toward their targets, the bombs shaking the earth as we sped on. We hit a curve and the back end fishtailed. Mickey said, "I can't see a goddamn thing," but he didn't slow down. I closed my eyes, laid my forehead against the cold window glass. Chief gave directions, the only one able to see in the darkness, the only one who knew what orders we had, what plans had been prepared for us. The rest of us didn't know where we were going or what would happen when we got there, but, like fools, we rushed on anyway.

ON FIRE

Modern scientific theory claims that the universe was born in fire: that at some silent signal an infinitesimally small, infinitesimally hot singularity began to expand or explode. The first planets were hot rocks sizzling through space. Burning gases united and formed the stars, and these stars drew planets around them, fire always at the center.

When our planet cooled enough to allow life, we crawled out of the primordial ooze, where the sun was waiting to warm us. We manufactured our first gods from the sun. They rode chariots, or boats, or winged creatures, and they hid at night, possibly in the darkness beneath the earth, but always they came back to draw the world in light.

In other words, we worshipped fire. God's first words in Genesis conjured fire, from which light sprang forth. To speak to Moses, God turned himself into fire. Plato writes of shadows in the light of a flickering fire forcing humanity to become self-aware, to seek reality and find illumination. Buddhist philosophy searches for an inner light.

It is not hard to see the beginnings of civilization in the light of a fire. Prehistoric man sits before a fire that flickers on the faces ringed around it. *Australopithecus* or Neanderthal stumbles upon fire from a lightning strike, holds his hands out for warmth. He takes a burning branch back to the cave. He piles on more wood. Fire then becomes a thing around which to gather while shadows flicker on the wall, sacred because it brings warmth and light. The idea of governance may have come from squatting around a fire while spitted meat burned, a place where men came together to discuss and discourse.

The first rule of survival is to find water or fire, depending on where you have become lost. It is not always the warmth you need but the psychological effect fire bestows. Warmth, yes, and light but also comfort, a pushing back of the darkness.

Creation then was a pushing back of darkness.

Which means that in the beginning, there was fire.

— — — — — — — — — — —

As a child I lived in fear of fire. Thirty miles from us stood Fort Chaffee, one of the largest live-fire forts in the country. Every weekend, bombs fell in the distance, rattling the windows in our house. The constant barrage sounded like thunder or some great cataclysm crawling out of the earth. At night, fighter jets streaked overhead, their red lights like fire drawn across the sky.

In the heat of summer, the fires began when the bombs ignited the dry Arkansas grass. Most of the time, fort personnel got the fires under control quickly, but some summers thick lines of smoke twisted skyward. Thirty miles away we could smell the smoke. Driving along the highways that circled the base, the air shimmered in the distance or thick screens of smoke rolled across the highway. At night the horizon glowed. The stars seemed distorted as the heat rose. Sometimes the fires could not be contained and marched ever closer to our house, the smoke thick enough to obscure the sun, and always I wondered what would happen if the fires could not be stopped.

Afterward the land lay scorched, the grass blackened and burned. Ash fell like snow. Trees smoldered for days. The fences along the roads occasionally trapped fleeing deer, their burned bodies twisted in the barbed wire or pushed against the chain link, eyes melted out of their heads, once-pink tongues hanging black out of mouths drawn back enough to expose the grayed teeth.

In fall and winter my father and I drove the endless back roads on cool mornings. Mist rose from the ponds and lakes, where deer would come down to drink. The hillsides had turned color to the fire of fall, and in forests of blackjack oak and scrub brush, the deer fled our approach, disappearing after only a brief flash of their white tails. We'd drive slowly, eyes scanning the land that emptied before us, often counting over a hundred, always fleeing, their instincts telling them that soon, again, would come a time of fire.

— — — — — — — — — — — —

At the Baptist church I went to, we heard constantly about hell, the fire awaiting us there. Our pastor rained down fire and brimstone from the pulpit, and the lake of burning sulfur shimmered before us like the highways outside Fort Chaffee.

We also feared what might fly through the skies from the Soviet Union. Heat lightning in summer made me afraid the bombs were falling and soon the sound would reach us, along with the blast wave. Our last lighted vision would be a mushroom cloud. I knew from my father watching the six o'clock news about SALT II and the Soviet invasion of Afghanistan that caused the United States to not sign. I knew from movies and TV how the missiles would soar skyward. They would disappear into our atmosphere, then strike, silently, and the world would become fire.

As prophesied.

— — — — — — — — — — — —

Prometheus was punished for bringing fire to man. He looked down from Mount Olympus and saw humans suffering and cold, living in caves, and it occurred to him that with fire they might progress from the caves and create cities and civilization.

But his contemporary gods deemed man too infallible to be trusted with such power. Man would either become strong and wise enough to challenge the gods or would destroy himself with such a dangerous tool. Fire, to them, was for gods alone.

But Prometheus did bring fire, defying Zeus. Carried it down the mountain on a burning brand. With fire, man was able to progress, to come forth from the caves.

Prometheus, as metaphor, stands for human achievement, the struggle to better our circumstances. He also stands as a warning of the dangers of power.

His punishment, then, was not for giving man the means to warm himself, or light his caves, or cook his food. It was for giving him the knowledge to destroy the world.

— — — — — — — — — — —

During the Spanish Inquisition, those thought to be witches were burned at the stake. People gathered in the center of town to watch, dressed in feast-day clothes. The law stated that victims were to be strangled before being burned, but many were not. They were tied to a stake and wood was piled around them, so all there could hear them burn, see their melting flesh (Catholic law forbade the spilling of blood, and, without flesh, they would have no form in the afterlife). Mostly women were burned at the stake, for the crime of heresy—which could mean anything from being able to adopt an animal form to being Protestant in a Catholic country.

In World War II the Soviet Union employed the scorched-earth strategy, fleeing before the Germans, burning everything as they went, so the German Army moved through a vast and desolate landscape where it could find neither food nor water. Russia had done the same thing a hundred years earlier, when Napoleon invaded. Sherman destroyed the South on his march to the sea.

After the atomic bombs were dropped, the ruins of Nagasaki and Hiroshima looked like the end of the world. Hundreds of thousands of Japanese were killed by fire. The dead lay burned in the street. Aerial photographs of the city show the ordered lines of streets, the carefully planned structure the city's creators built, but there are no people, no buildings. There is no city, only a world reduced to waste.

Firefighters use the word "containment" when arriving at a fire, a word that captures our ancient fear of fire—if we cannot stop it, we must not let it spread. Even the way a fire is fought emphasizes the idea—the fire must first be contained, and only then can it be controlled, then weakened, then extinguished, the whole process following a natural, logical order.

In the early 70s, the first nuclear arms talks began between the Soviet Union and the United States. Our hoards of nuclear weapons, now no longer only bombs but ICBMs that could reach across the world, had become too large, and the two countries began to talk about containing them, as if someone had looked to the future and saw the land ravaged by black fire, our lakes boiling and expanding under waves of superheat, the whole thing spreading to engulf the world.

When my stepfather crossed the desert in the winter of 1991, in the early days of the ground war in the Gulf, Saddam Hussein's troops had already lit the oil wells. Black smoke spewed into the sky. The horizon lay lit like sunset, like the last days of the earth, he told me. They rode in darkness, with only the fires for company. Hundreds of miles this way, he said, only oily yellow flames in the distance, the smell of burning sulfur, the vast and empty landscape.

Close to Baghdad they began to take on enemy fire. My stepfather's unit shot eight-inch-diameter shells from howitzer cannons and in only a few minutes had fallen into line and began to return fire. The night lit up with explosions. The world became fire, he said, the night turned into day in brief flashes, and with each explosion came heat and noise, the ground shaking beneath them.

A few miles behind them, a battalion of multiple launch rocket systems had set up and was firing over their heads, and when a missile went past, the red trail of its ignition system lit the world like hell. In its wake, they could see each other's faces.

For weeks they crossed the desert, always finding the remains of fire—trucks and tanks with blacked-out interiors, tongues of black where flames spilled out of windows. They passed small villages where the Iraqi military had hunkered down, and though occasionally a soldier appeared from a deep bunker with his hands held out in front of him, mostly they found the ravages of fire from the bombs that had been falling for months.

In the distance, the oil fires still burned. At the end of each day, he told me, with sunset flaming the rim of the world, you could not tell what was fire and what was supposed to be there.

— — — — — — — — — — —

The Cuyahoga River in Cleveland has caught fire at least thirteen times since the 1860s. The Buffalo, Rouge, and Chicago Rivers have all caught fire as well, due to either piles of debris or pollution such as oil and industrial waste. Imagine seeing a river on fire, flames boiling from the surface, like the fabled lake in hell. This seems extraordinary to me—that we have created a way for water to burn.

— — — — — — — — — — —

According to the International Fire Service Training Association, there are four stages to a fire: incipiency, growth, full development, and decay. All seem to me analogous to human life: the soul as spark, inception as conception, then growth, and decay a sliding toward death until the final spark is extinguished. They might also be the stages of the cycle of the earth, though we have not yet reached fully developed, or decay.

I wonder at what point a fire is considered out of control, or unstoppable, but neither of those phrases seem to enter into the official lexicon. The closest we get is a five-alarm fire, which means that anyone anywhere near the vicinity of the fire needs to respond right fucking now.

——— ——— ——— ——— ——— ——— ——— ——— ——— ——— ———

An early memory: somewhere, not our house, someone is cooking, an older child—thirteen or fourteen—but not an adult. The grease in the pan catches fire, and flames erupt toward the ceiling, three or four feet high, black smoke curling against the oven hood. The fire spreads over the stove. Whoever is cooking calmly reaches for sugar and dumps it onto the flames, and the rest of the day the kitchen smells like burnt sugar, but a crisis has been averted. Only later did I learn that had the person used water to try to extinguish the flames, the entire house might have burned.

——— ——— ——— ——— ——— ——— ——— ——— ——— ——— ———

When I joined the military, my National Guard unit summer camped at Fort Chaffee, closer now to the bombs I had been hearing all my life, closer to the source of the distant fires I had watched from my bedroom window late at night, the light above the tops of the trees like false dawn. On base we could hear heavy artillery firing constantly, knocking plaster loose from the ceilings of the old barracks. Sometimes a particularly violent round, or one that had gotten off course and landed too close, shook our beds hard, and some nights we woke wondering what had just happened, a ringing in our ears that should not have been there.

My second or third day on Chaffee, before we moved to the woods and set up our tents and camouflaged netting and pretended that war had come for real and that the planes flying overhead were looking for us, my boss drove me out to the .50-caliber range. He was a full-time warrant officer with almost thirty years in the guard and had arranged for me to fire one of the heavy machine guns.

When I climbed up on the armored personnel carrier where the machine gun was mounted, heat swam in the distance. Dirt fountained upward on the distant hills as the fighters dropped their bombs, and it was not hard to pretend that war had come. When I pressed the triggers, dirt and dust blew up far downrange. An old tank, placed there for target practice, erupted in sparks where the bullets struck.

Downrange, the grass caught fire. The summer sun had drawn all the moisture out of the ground, and the shrubs and grasses had turned brown and yellow. The tracers, bullets with phosphorus embedded in them so the rifle operator can see where he is firing, had ignited the dry grasses, and in only a few seconds a brush fire sprang up. In the July heat, the fire spread quickly. We radioed back to base for fire personnel but could do nothing more, only watch the fire grow.

The wind kicked up as the fire came closer, the heat stirring the air, whipping it around. Ash rose into the swirling air as a two- or three-hundred-foot-high tornado grew from the wind of the fire. I could hear it, not like the real tornados that dropped from spring storms but a low moaning, like the voice of fire. There was an ambulance nearby, and as the firenado came for us, I dove in the back. The fire followed me into the ambulance, swirling gauze and bandages around, ash thick in the confined space. Sparks landed on my skin. The smoke caught in the back of my throat. My eyes watered and stung.

After a moment it was over. The fire was already burning itself out in the sparse landscape. Base fire personnel came and stomped out the last of it. The tornado dispersed as the fire lost intensity. In a few minutes everything was over, and we started firing again.

— — — — — — — — — — —

My house in North Carolina is two blocks from a fire station. From the frequency of fire trucks leaving the station, there seem to be thousands of fires in this city, though I have never seen one. I only hear the siren whine as the engines fire up and roar out of the station and onto the street, the sound blasting through my open windows in spring and summer, then fading into the distance. When we first moved here, the sirens would wake me late at night, and I would lie in bed and imagine fire and flames, but now I don't even hear them. I suppose a person can get used to anything.

— — — — — — — — — — —

My grandparents were married on December 6, 1941, and woke the next morning to learn about the bombing of Pearl Harbor. On the radio, Roosevelt gave his address about a day that will live in infamy and immediately fired up the American war machine. While the men were being shipped to the Pacific or European theaters, Rosie the Riveter stepped into the factories. My grandfather fought in the Battle of the Bulge but lived to tell about it. Not long after, he marched into Berlin and met the Russians there, our allies whom we would soon decide we really didn't like very much, and war of a different sort would begin.

Sunday afternoons he'd tell me stories of Normandy, the Battle of the Bulge, cold nights in German forests. The streets of Paris, France, when the city was liberated. The ruins of Dresden and Berlin. From Fort Chaffee less than thirty miles away the bombs would be falling like old thunder, old war.

If the attack on Pearl Harbor is the defining date of my grandfather's generation, and JFK's assassination my father's, then September 11, 2001, belongs to mine: the Twin Towers on fire, then falling, the great clouds of smoke and dust billowing through lower Manhattan. I'm surprised that no tagline like the aforementioned "A day that will live in infamy" has been attached. Maybe we just have less time for infamy nowadays, and the abbreviated "9/11" works just as well as any speech. Or perhaps those images of the Twin Towers falling need no assigned appellation because the repercussions are still rebounding inside us, and a designation for that sad moment of our lives does not need any added emphasis, or the fire caused by those four airplanes any multiplier.

——— ——— ——— ——— ——— ——— ——— ——— ——— ——— ———

On days when the guns weren't firing, we often drove across Fort Chaffee on our way to Fort Smith, which was once a frontier fort on the edge of Indian territory but is no longer, only a city of some eighty or ninety thousand people.

On the north side of Chaffee stood the old barracks, and driving past on our way into Fort Smith we could see the long straight rows, windows filmed over like ancient eyes. The barracks were begun in 1941, as the U.S. Army prepared for war, and the first soldiers arrived on December 7, right about the time fire began to fall on Pearl Harbor. Elvis Presley lived in the barracks for a few days on his way to Fort Hood in 1958. Cuban refugees were housed there in the 80s, fleeing from the disorder in their own country—three weeks after arriving, the refugees rioted and burned several of the buildings.

I spent summers in those barracks in the early 90s. Walking through the empty buildings, I was reminded of the number of men who had passed through here on their way to war, the number of people who had been housed here after fleeing war and fire and civil disorder, or whatever it was that had destroyed the world in which they had lived.

In early 2008, a fire started in one of the buildings and spread quickly, going from incipiency to growth and staying there for some time. Firefighters used bulldozers to cut firebreaks to prevent the fire from spreading, but fifty-miles-per-hour winds

pushed it into other buildings. The old wood went up like kin-
dling. There are videos on YouTube now of people driving along
the stretch of Arkansas Highway 22 that ran close to the barracks, and you can see the black smoke and flames rising from
the buildings, spreading quickly, as if the fire I had so long
feared had finally come.

Over 150 buildings burned. All that was left of the old
barracks were the stone chimneys, smoking and smoldering. In 2011, on the hottest day ever recorded at Fort Chaffee, another fire broke out and burned most of the buildings
that remained.

Much of the land now has been returned to the cities of Fort
Smith and Barling. No permanent military troops are stationed
there. But in the summer, Arkansas National Guard troops
come back to train. The Air Guard drops bombs on Razorback
Range, shaking the earth and the houses all around. The buildings are gone, as are the gateposts and the fences that once
surrounded the fort, but every summer the soldiers return and
the fires begin again.

When my brother and I were little, we used to burn army men.
I don't know what got into us sometimes. We'd buy bags of little
green army men in various poses, men with rifles and bazookas
and flame-throwers, then line them all up on a low rock wall
behind our house and pose them in defensive positions. My
brother would produce a lighter and a can of hairspray.

"Die, Russians," he would say, moving down the line of men,
using the hairspray as a torch. "Die, commies," he said as they
caught fire.

After we'd killed the Russians, we would burn our cowboys
and Indians indiscriminately, their past differences forgotten,
and once, after we had run out of everyone else, my brother
brought out our collection of *Star Wars* figures and burned
them, starting with the Dark Side—Darth Vader and Boba

Fett and the stormtroopers—and then progressing to our heroes: Han Solo and Princess Leia and the ultimate defender of the Light, Luke Skywalker. I cried when my brother did this. I begged him to stop, but none of my entreaties to his sense of humanity worked. Many years later it occurred to me that after we'd burned all the men from Earth, we started burning those who lived among the stars.

——— ——— ——— ——— ——— ——— ——— ——— ——— ——— ———

How angry the gods must have been at Prometheus. Angry enough to chain him to the mountain, an eagle eating his insides for all time. But they must have been afraid as well, and fear often drives our anger, so sometimes I wonder why they did not punish him with fire. It seems more fitting.

FELDGRAU

Feldgrau is a German word, translated to "field gray," the color of the uniforms of the Wehrmacht and the Waffen and the Luftwaffe or the color of those old films of the siege of Stalingrad.

It was also the color of the Bundeswehr, the West German army, after the country was split in half. This was before the wall went up in Berlin and the old alliances were severed, lines drawn. Before the airlift and the Cold War and the theory that if the nukes ever flew, the world would turn gray as nuclear winter set in when the smoke from the burning would obscure the sun.

This, of course, was after World War II. After the Maginot Line and Dunkirk and the Battle of the Bulge. After the fire-bombing of Dresden and the two mushroom clouds rising over Japan.

But before everything else that happened happened.

In my mind, it is the color of mountains or the uniforms we wear in them now as the report of rifles echoes down into the valleys. It is the color of the streets of Kabul or Kandahar, where men wary and weary from watching everything that approaches close their eyes at night and see only gray. In the airport on my way to Chicago I saw these uniforms everywhere, as if the men wearing them were traveling or returning from all corners of the earth, and on the airplane I inspected the colors of the soldier I sat by, the way the greens and grays blended so that he seemed to disappear even there on the seat high above the earth, although he didn't really disappear until we got off the plane.

Colors are made to camouflage, to hide men from other men, to make it, at short glance, hard to tell a man apart from a rock or the earth or the distant trees in the last stretch of forest, to make it easy to erase one's presence. All war is landscape, our uniforms tell us—they only change depending on where we walk, where we war.

— — — — — — — — — — — —

The gray is not gray but some other color. It looks to me like winter. Like cold winds over a leached landscape. Like those old films again, tanks tumbling over frozen earth, the Russians retreating, all England hiding in the subways as the bombs erupt night after night and London burns. It looks like the smoke from burning jungles bombed by napalm or the windswept flanks of mountains while blue smoke rises in the valleys.

It is the color of the mass graves my grandfather found in Korea, only the ground had frozen so hard it wasn't so much graves covering the bodies as gravity holding them to earth. It is the color the bodies might have turned or the color of the TV screen when I watch what used to be war, where gray is the color of ruptured cities with crumbling buildings, the color of the film, the color of the room I find myself watching from late at night while everyone else is asleep.

— — — — — — — — — — — —

In our back closet, my father's jungle camo had our same name sewn over the heart, and I took this to heart on days I snuck into his room to wear his skin over mine, to gain his smell of starch and aftershave, to walk in his polished boots. My grandfather's gear from World War II was OD green, which means, in military language, olive drab, and I should have something to say about that, some comment on the difference of those two words, one a live thing, the other with connotations of darkness and depression, but I do not. Only that it hung in the back room, hidden behind the suits he wore to church and the suits he wore to work, the big red "1" stitched to the shoulder like blood.

When my stepfather was called to war we were in a new arena, and his colors were sand and desert, the colors of the storms that came spinning out of the Middle East, turning the desert moon red as blood. When I joined the military, my uniform had my father's name sewn right where he had once worn mine, and though he had already walked in my boots, I do not know what he thought to see a younger version of himself wearing what he had once worn, as if the past had circled back to the present, as if we were always at war.

These uniforms hung in our houses like the thin skins of empty men. As if only their shells had returned.

— — — — — — — — — — —

The *feldgrau* uniform was last used by the West German army in 1958. It is not a specific color but a blend of grays and browns more suitable to modern warfare than the bright blues and brilliant reds of the nineteenth century, when men would stand shoulder to shoulder and only fire when they saw the whites of the enemies' eyes.

It is close to the color of the Iraqi hat my stepfather brought back from Desert Storm. The one I still have hidden away, the one I will sometimes bring out to show friends if we have gotten drunk enough under the spinning stars and the talk has turned to what wars we are still engaged in or what wars linger in our collective past, and when I bring it out they turn it in their hands for some time, not speaking, just turning it again and again as I tell the story of how my stepfather saw it lifting in the hot desert wind as his battalion rolled toward Baghdad, how he leaned from the truck and snatched it on the move as it skittered over the sand, and when I stop talking, my friends will finally look up and ask, "What color is that?" because they need words that ignore the bloodstain and the bullet hole centered in the forehead.

ESSAY IN FIVE PHOTOGRAPHS

1

It was after Korea.

He is dressed in his service uniform. There are insignia sewn on the shoulder, but he is facing the camera, one arm draped over my uncle, and I cannot make the insignia out. My uncle is holding my mother. She has black hair and one tiny arm raised, her fist clenched. She is less than a year old.

In the picture behind them is a screen door and the face of a brick building. The metal letters on the screen door say it is apartment 10 C. I know that this must be in Fort Benning, Georgia, in 1951 or '52. My uncle is a young boy, his pants legs rolled up. My mother is asleep.

The picture was taken ten years after he was married—ten years after he woke the morning following his wedding and learned that the Japanese had attacked Pearl Harbor. Probably seven years since he landed on the beaches of Normandy sometime in July 1944. Seven years—longer than my uncle had been alive—since the bullets streaked by and the bombs fell all around during the Battle of the Bulge, when he must have knelt, twenty-eight years old then, his wife and son halfway around the world, his M1 carbine shaking in his hands as he returned fire, hoping the bombs and bullets did not find him, hoping that he would see his wife and son again.

It would have been only a few years since he was called to Korea. He thought his fighting days were done, but his National Guard unit was activated and he was asked to take up arms again. This time there was a daughter he was leaving behind as well, but he did not know that then—she was only a fertilized egg forming somewhere in my grandmother's womb.

The picture does not show the wound where the bayonet stabbed his knee in Korea. It does not show the strokes that would make it difficult for him to walk, nor does it show the fierce pain that would grip his heart late one night, taking away his speech, his movement, and a few hours later, his life. In the picture he is young, a soldier returned home from war sitting on the steps of a rented apartment with his arm around his oldest son, who is holding a daughter he is meeting for the first time. It does show the grin on his face at seeing his daughter—my mother. At the fact that, after returning from war, here was a child, one fist raised to welcome him home.

2

In this picture, my father looks like me.

The resemblance is strong. But this picture was taken in 1967, five years before I was born. Right around the time he met my mother, both of them young then, my mother still in high school. The draft was just firing up, ghostly images of Vietnam appearing on TV screens all over the country, and more and more men were being shipped to a small country many of them had never heard of, from which many of them would never return.

It sits on a shelf at my grandmother's small apartment, where she moved after my grandfather passed. Around it are pictures of aunts and uncles I rarely see anymore, cousins and nieces and nephews that I have never met. But my eyes are drawn to my father, a child himself then, his hat tilted at what seems a jaunty angle. It would have been taken at Fort Polk, Louisiana, where he learned to shoot dummies with an M16 and stab dummies with a bayonet and throw hand grenades at other dummies, or it might have been at Fort Sam Houston in Texas, where, as a battlefield medic, he learned to triage whatever damage had been done by enemies wielding rifles and bayonets and hand grenades.

His hair is cropped close, face clean-shaven. His shoulders are narrow and bony, the same as mine were at that age. His eyes are a deep blue, the same as mine, the same as both my daughters'. His ears look too large for his head, though the picture does not show how, eventually, he will grow out of the awkwardness of youth.

The picture also does not show signs of worry. It seems it would. But there are none. Just my father, a slight grin on his face, as if this is all somehow amusing, as if he did not see the nights and days before him when he would worry over the prospect of war as the numbers of men in Vietnam continued to escalate. He would marry my mother, still worrying if, at any time, his unit would be activated, seeing friends drafted, knowing sometimes only their names and their flag-draped coffins came back.

He tells me that many men like him were joining National Guard units as a way to avoid Vietnam without moving to Canada. He was struggling then, from a poor family, so when he joined, the money was welcome. He stayed for over twenty years, long after he married my mother, long after my brother and then I came along. Long after the divorce and a long litany of military actions in other parts of the world that too many people have never heard of: Libya and Lebanon and Latin America,

Grenada and the Philippines and Panama, Colombia and Bo-
livia and Peru.

When I am eighteen he will tell me that serving was good for
him. I will join his National Guard unit, and while I am at Basic
Training I will have a picture taken in the same pose, almost
the same uniform, the same small smile on my face, though I
can see now that the smile is not one of amusement but rather
uncertainty, wondering what all this—the uniform, the rifle I
will be issued later, everything I've heard about unstable forces
at large in the world—might someday mean.

3

Almost twenty years later, I'm surprised at how young I look.

This was long before I married, had children, slipped quietly into my forties. Long before I learned the names of the
various conflicts that seem to always be ongoing or just starting up, rarely ending. I had just graduated high school. The
army jacket I am wearing is not mine. I have no name tag,
no dog tags. I might be an unknown soldier. The brass and
insignia are generic, and at this point I do not even know what
they mean.

The picture is a public relations picture, taken only a few
days after I arrive at Fort Sill. They buzz our heads and dress
us from the shoulders up and snap our pictures, then send the
pictures home to our parents and girlfriends with a generic note
saying we are doing well, adjusting to military life, and that we
will write as soon as our duties allow.

Which we do. We write every evening, sending letters to
everyone we know, and, slowly at first, then with increasing
volume, we get letters back. We get letters from parents telling
us how proud they are of us, our fathers recalling their days
in the army or else lamenting the flat feet that kept them out.
We get letters from buddies telling us about trips to the lake,
drinking beer on a Sunday afternoon, and, closed up in the

barracks as night falls around us, we can almost taste the beer in the backs of our throats, smell the lake, boats cutting white froths through the blue water. We get letters from girlfriends, and sometimes the letters include pictures of them in bathing suits or bras and panties, sometimes nothing at all.

We run the letters over and over in our minds. During the few moments we have each night to read our mail we memorize the curves of girlfriends and the words that accompany the letters, translating "I can't wait to see you" into our own fantasies, and through the long days of training we recall the words and images. During the short nights, we dream of going home, reconstructing our elaborate fantasies about what will happen when we get back there, until morning comes too early and we wake dreading the coming day, stalking wearily through it. When night falls again we mark the day off our calendars with much ceremony and pass around the pictures our girlfriends sent us, the pictures our parents sent of our cars or our dogs or our high school football team, anything that connects us with what we have left behind.

Because we have no contact with the outside world. Only the letters, a few pictures, a phone call once a week on Sunday morning. We have no idea what forces are stirring in the Middle East. This is late summer 1990, and we are trudging through our days, firing M16s and thinking of breasts and black panties, when Saddam Hussein invades Kuwait. Within days, the 82nd Airborne and the 1st Marine Expeditionary Force are mobilized, and just two weeks after the United Nations Security Council passes Resolution 660, condemning the invasion and demanding the immediate withdrawal of all Iraqi troops, we are scheduled to graduate. We have completed Basic Rifle Marksmanship and hand-to-hand combat. We have thrown live hand grenades and stabbed dummies with bayonets. We have navigated through the darkness clutching our rifles and covered our heads when trip flares exploded into the night, and just before we graduate we take another picture, this one of the whole platoon, though we still seem, looking at it now, far too young.

4

It was after the Gulf War.

The platoon in the picture is C Battery, 2nd/ 142nd Field Artillery, Arkansas National Guard. They wear desert camos with a razorback on the shoulder, the insignia of the University of Arkansas's sports teams. On the other shoulder is an insignia that looks exactly like a vibrator, and that is what the men in the unit call it, but it is actually a representation of the eight-inch-diameter shells they fire from howitzer artillery pieces, great cannons that can launch shells over twenty miles through the desert air and rain down death on an enemy that can't even see where the fire is coming from.

Their uniforms are dirty. They have been traveling for days: first the long flights from Riyadh to Germany to Maine to Little Rock, then a two-hour bus ride back to their unit, where placards and signs and yellow ribbons waved as the Greyhounds pulled in and spilled them out into the Arkansas night.

My stepfather is in the back, off to the right side. If you look closely, you can see a few beer cans half-hidden by the men holding them. One or two of them look already drunk, eyes slightly glassed over. But they are smiling, and one man in the back has his beer can half-raised, and several of the others are glancing off to the side, to somewhere you cannot see in the picture, but where I know their families are looking on as the picture is snapped.

They have been home from Iraq for less than an hour. Right after the picture is taken they will break apart and their families will take them home, and it will not be until later, when they have taken off their uniforms, that their wives will see how much weight they have lost. You cannot tell in the picture.

Nor can you tell what will happen next. If they will go silent on the ride home. Break down crying. Wake in the middle of the night with cold sweats. Or simply sleep, everything forgotten now that it is done. In a few days they will reassemble and begin checking their gear, writing lists of what needs to be repaired and reordered and reevaluated, preparing for what happens next, and when they see this preparation, many of the men in the unit, my stepfather among them, will retire, unable or unwilling to do it again.

5

About the last pictures, I can only guess. There are thousands of dead in the war now, and hundreds of thousands going back through time, through Desert Storm and Vietnam and all the little wars and excursions and missions in between, Korea and both the world wars and a hundred or a thousand or a million others.

Now, you can find their faces easily enough. They stare at you from newspapers, on the internet and TV, from billboards along the highway where you are rushing to work in the morning. Their names are printed beneath them. They look young, usually, though not always. They have dark hair or light hair, blue eyes or brown. They played football in high school, had girlfriends they would marry as soon as they returned. Or perhaps they would decide to go to college and earn a degree. They might have children already, a dark-haired girl with the same color eyes as her father, or a blond child with her mother's hands, or a boy that resembled a grandfather who died in some other war long ago.

For the most part, they are stoic. Trying to be strong, to act as they believe soldiers should act, to look as they believe soldiers should look. Some of them are smiling. That seems even worse, now that they are dead. There are a few women among them, and because I have two daughters, their faces stay with me, even though I try not to remember their names. They are marines or army or air force or navy, privates or corporals or staff sergeants or second lieutenants, though never generals, and they joined for college money or because they were poor or because they wanted to serve their country.

But this is only speculation.

As is what the pictures don't show. How they were excited or scared or anxious or proud when they first joined the military. How they suffered or excelled during training, barely qualifying or graduating with flying colors or anywhere in between. How they sat up late at night watching the twenty-four-hour news when the war first began, talking quietly about what might happen, or waiting to use the phone and call home, or driving home and making love to their wife or husband, playing with their child.

How they landed in the desert. Went on patrol. Were blown up by a roadside bomb or shot through the throat by a sniper. Their dog tags were recovered. Someone said a few words. Their flag-draped bodies were flown home and unloaded in the dead of night on some anonymous tarmac. A mother woke to a ringing phone, holding her breath as a father reached for the receiver. A few days later she flinched each of the three times the seven guns fired. The flag fell from her hands.

Later, she turned the pages in a scrapbook she'd made of her son or daughter's life. She tried to show it to a boy or a girl that would grow up without a mother or a father, or a husband who had to go on living without a wife, or a wife without a husband, a father without a son, a mother without a daughter.

In my mind, the child is too young to look at the pictures. Too young to understand what they mean. The child is smiling. One fist is raised. It will be years before the child understands, if ever.

But, as I said, all this is only speculation. I don't know. I wasn't there, like almost all of us.

THE HORNET AMONG US

The Japanese giant hornet is not the largest insect in the world but perhaps the most fierce. It can grow to two inches in length, with a wingspan of three. It has a brown thorax and a yellow-and-brown-striped abdomen. Its mandibles are jagged, lined with sharp, incisor-like protrusions. Its eyes are large dark holes, which make it seem alien, some thing that has no place in our ordered world.

It can fly sixty miles in a day at speeds of over twenty-five miles an hour. Its wings beat about a thousand times a minute. It can lift more weight, relative to size, than any of us can imagine. Its stinger is a quarter of an inch long and barbless, which means it can sting repeatedly. Its venom can melt human flesh. The venom is loaded with at least eight different chemicals, some of which damage tissue, some of which cause pain, and at least one that's sole purpose is to attract other hornets to do more stinging.

Here's how the hornets work: Scouts zoom around searching for honeybee hives. This is all they do from when they wake in the spring to when they hibernate in the fall. When a scout finds a hive, it leaves pheromone markers around it, which draw other hornets. When the others arrive, they begin systematically slaughtering the bees. A Japanese giant hornet can kill forty honeybees in an hour. A nest of Japanese giant hornets, around thirty or so, can destroy an entire honeybee colony in a few hours. The hornets seize the bees one by one and literally slice them apart. They cut off their heads and limbs and wings and keep the juicy, most nutrient-rich parts, which they chew into a paste to feed to their larvae. They eat the bees' honey and devour their young. They do not take over the bees' hives or carefully consume all they have killed. They take only the flight muscles and other juicy bits and leave the heads and limbs lying around.

——— —— —— —— —— —— ——— —— —— ——

Hornets' nests are founded by a queen in a dark sheltered place, either underground or in the hollow of a tree. The fertilized queen creates cells from chewed-up tree bark and lays an egg in each cell. The queen spends her entire life laying eggs. The eggs transform into larvae, and the larvae spin silk over the openings in their cells. In two weeks they complete metamorphosis and hatch. The first generation is workers. They hatch from fertilized eggs and are female. The females take over construction of the hive. They spend their time tending to the home, caring for the young, shoring up walls, and feeding. Unfertilized eggs become males. The males are called scouts, or drones. They spend their entire lives searching for bees' nests to destroy.

——— —— —— —— —— —— ——— —— —— ——

Fully formed nests of the Japanese giant hornet are the size of a small child. They can have hundreds of workers. The workers are smaller than the queen but very aggressive to intruders. Recently, population growth in Japan, and the resulting decimation of the Japanese giant hornet's forest habitat, has caused a population growth in the yellow hornet. The yellow hornet has moved into the cities of Japan, where it drinks from discarded soft drink cans and pilfers trash for leftover food. Over forty people a year die from its stings.

The Japanese giant hornet has no natural predators except man. In Japan, they are a delicacy. They are eaten raw or deep-fried, or the amino acids on which they live are harvested and manufactured into a sports energy drink.

The Japanese honeybee does have a defense against the giant hornet, though it does not always work. Sometimes it fails and the bees are destroyed, their heads ripped off and their children eaten and the remains of their bodies strewn about the hive they once called home.

But if the bees are quick enough, if they act according to the plan created for them over millions of years, here is what they do: when a scout appears, they wait until the last possible second, the last instant before it spreads its pheromones, before it summons the army that will destroy the hive.

At some unspoken sign, some chemical signal like a flare going off in the night, the bees surround the hornet scout so tightly it cannot get away. As one, they begin vibrating their bodies. They rattle themselves so hard that they begin to heat up, to burn inside, to turn themselves to fire. Because the bees can withstand higher temperatures than the hornet, the hornet dies. It inevitably kills a few of the bees before it does, but the hive is saved.

The Old English word *hyrnetu* means "large wasp, beetle." The Middle English *harnete* was probably influenced by the word "horn," either as "horner," to suggest the sting, or "horn blower," to suggest the buzz.

In the Hebrew, the word *tsir'ah* means "stinging." In Exodus 23:28, God told Moses, "And I will send hornets before you, which shall drive out the Hivite, the Canaanite, and the Hittite."

Deuteronomy 7:20 tells us, "Moreover the LORD your God will send the hornet among them until those who are left, who hide themselves from you, are destroyed," and Joshua 24:12 says, "I sent the hornet before you which drove them out from before you . . . *but* not with your sword or with your bow."

Biblical scholars believe the word "hornet" is not literal. In the first two verses, it is a metaphor for panic, a physical manifestation of the fear of the wrath of God. In Joshua, the word "hornet" means "army."

— — — — — — — — — — —

Army ants also spend much of their lives searching for things to destroy. Like an army, they raid in swarms or columns, depending on the species of ant. In swarms, great fans of raiders sweep along the ground searching for food. Column raiders branch out in small foraging groups, but both techniques utilize overwhelming numbers to envelop prey. Both rely on chemical trails to organize, like orders sent ahead. Both are deadly effective.

While the ants are raiding, birds follow along, eating the flying insects the ants flush from the ground. The larger colonies of ants eat up to 100,000 prey animals each day. They kill lizards and scorpions and centipedes. They kill grasshoppers and mantises and spiders. When they encounter prey, they simply swarm over them. The venom in their stings liquefies the victims' tissues. They cut the bodies into pieces to carry. Some species swarm trees and eat small birds and their eggs. Others hunt mainly the nests of other ant species and wasps. Still others hunt underground, devouring worms and arthropods and young vertebrates.

Because of how much they consume, the ants must migrate. They are constantly moving into new territory, constantly flushing prey, swarming over it, destroying, and dismembering. Larger animals that they cannot consume are killed anyway and left to rot, the ants leaving a swath of death in their wake.

Like an army, they hunt while they move. Soldiers link their bodies to form protective barriers or use their large mandibles to guard the smaller workers while they sting their prey. Scouts constantly search for more prey, laying chemical trails, marking the path for the colony to follow. Other scouts split off from the group to forage or to find a new home for the night. When they move, they take everything with them: food, larvae, eggs, and the queen, who is too big to walk and must be carried.

Army ants belong to the subfamily of ants called Dorylinae, after the Greek word for "spear." Their colonies can contain 20 million ants and function as a superorganism. There is no one controlling intelligence. They act out of instinct, driven by chemical composition. Only the queen can see. The workers are all blind. Millions of years of convergent evolution have led the ants to this point. They march along the forest floor destroying everything in their path, each mind alike, each behavior the same.

— — — — — — — — — — — —

There is a wasp in certain parts of the world that paralyzes its prey, usually a spider, and lays its egg in the paralyzed body, which it buries alive. When the egg hatches, the larva feeds on the body of the spider. The spider is alive as the larva eats it. It can do nothing to get away. Its stomach is eaten. Its eyes are eaten. Its body is eaten, and after the larva has devoured all the edible parts of the spider, it spins a silk cocoon and pupates.

There is a spider that uses a handheld net to scoop up prey. It folds itself into a stick, blending in with real sticks, and lies in wait a few inches above the ground, net ready. When prey wanders by, it unfolds itself from the stick and scoops its little net down and wraps its prey up.

There is a species of fire ant that builds rafts. Thousands of ants lock themselves together, and they go floating gently down the stream. The ones on the bottom die, but the colony survives. These fire ants were indigenous to South America but have now invaded the Philippines, China, and the southern United States. They have no natural predators. When they attack, they first bite, digging in with their mandibles, to make themselves hard to remove. Then they sting again and again with stingers left over from a million years ago, when they evolved from wasps.

There is a species of spider that mimics ants so it won't be eaten. There is a species of ant that creates traps like a spider, and when prey appears, the ants spring from hiding and pull the prey's legs off so that it cannot run away. There is a species of centipede that is covered with spines and shoots cyanide from its mouth. There is a species of centipede that can grow as long as your forearm. There is a species of bug in Africa that subsists on blood. When it mates, it stabs the female in the abdomen to release sperm directly into her bloodstream, and the female has had to evolve, over the years, a defense so that reproducing won't kill her.

——— —— —— —— —— —— —— —— —— —— ——

Ingenious the ways in which nature kills. The ant wears armor. The wasp wields a sword and attacks from the skies. The spider creates elaborate traps for its prey. The hornet works in teams; the ant works in armies so vast numbers lose meaning. Even the lowly bee has developed measures of counterattack.

They have all evolved, over millions of years, the ability to destroy. This means it was something they worked at. They got better and better and better, and they are good at what they do.

There is only one animal that is better and has worked harder.

—— —— —— —— —— —— —— —— —— —— ——

When Rome fell to the barbarians, while the city was sacked and burned, while a thousand years of darkness set upon the Western world, someone, looking at everything he had ever known fall, must have thought that the invaders in all their glorious multitudes looked like swarming ants. When Masada was surrounded, one of the besieged surely believed the Romans were hornets, alien, so far removed from humanity that they were of another world. When the Greeks stood at the narrow neck of Thermopylae, they must have seen the hordes coming for them, wave after wave after wave, as nonsentient, some form of mindless drone. And when the airplanes lit the night skies over Baghdad, a child, huddled in a corner somewhere, certainly believed that some creature from nightmare, from legend or lore or myth, had arisen like a prophecy.

But in their secret hearts they must have known what was coming for them, must have seen, somewhere in the collective conscious, soldiers marching along dusty roads and cities at siege and the dead in the streets. They must have known the feel of tanks rumbling over the earth and the sound of airplanes droning through the skies. They must have seen, in our past and present and future, black lines of smoke twisting toward the clouds as the spear was raised and the sword fell and the hordes came from the mists on the river, howling and rattling their shields, the hornet driven before them.

CHICKEN

The night I deployed, four inches of ice fell across the state of Arkansas. This was late December, in the dark days right after Christmas. My friends and I were home from the various colleges we'd escaped to after high school, and in the few days before we disappeared again we drank too much and woke in the cold mornings hurting in a hundred different ways. A fine mist fell through the streetlights, and already the temperature was dropping.

Four or five of us were playing pool in a dive bar when my mother walked in. She looked on the verge of crying. Two years before, she'd seen her husband deployed to Desert Storm, and she'd just received a phone call with a similar code word—in this case "Roaring Bull"—which meant my National Guard unit had been mobilized.

"I don't know what it's about," she told me, near tears. "They wouldn't say over the phone."

When the call came for my stepfather to go to Desert Storm—still Desert Shield at the time—we knew why without asking. We'd been watching the news for months, since Hussein invaded Kuwait, and we didn't need to decipher any code words to know my stepfather was being sent to the Middle East. The entire U.S. Army had been sent, it seemed, all except my guard unit. For the two years since the Gulf War ended, I had been telling people I wish I would have gone too, but that night, my mother crying in a shitty pool hall where sad country music played endlessly on the 60s jukebox, I would have given anything to be out of the guard.

Outside, the rain had turned to sleet. We didn't know it then, but north of us, in the Ozark Mountains, the rain had turned to sleet hours ago. Already a layer of ice was covering trees and roads and power lines, and already electrical grids were going dark.

I drove straight to the National Guard armory, leaving my mother and my friends standing in the sleet shivering. In the turning-slick parking lot, I slid into a spot and climbed out breathing on my hands. A half dozen guard members were standing in a circle, wondering what was happening. We all looked strange without our uniforms on. Most of these were middle-aged men, going slowly bald and fat, and none of us looked like soldiers. I was still too young, my shoulders thin as knife blades, and like most young men, too assured of my own importance.

Our voices echoed in the empty space of the big drill hall as we went in. We could hear the sleet hitting the roof, harder now. We still didn't know what was coming. We never do. One moment you're shooting pool and getting slowly drunk, and the next you're looking to see what's falling from the sky. That's the way it's always been and, I suspect, always will be.

By the time First Sergeant Thomas called us to attention, another two dozen men had arrived. Some of them had shaved and dressed—the rest of us stood in our civilian clothes. In northwest Arkansas, Thomas told us, the ice had knocked out electricity. It would only get worse, he said. The ice line was creeping farther south every minute as the night deepened and the cold came on. By morning, he said, there would be no power anywhere.

"So we're supposed to keep people alive?" someone asked.

Thomas shook his head. "People can take care of themselves," he said. "They have wood stoves, fireplaces, blankets. We have to"—and I'll say he smiled and shook his head slightly, like even our superiors knew how absurd this was—"save the chickens."

Tyson Foods, headquartered in Springdale, Arkansas, is the world's second largest processor and marketer of meat in the world. Chicken and turkey houses litter the countryside of Arkansas, and when the ice came down the chicken industry stood to lose hundreds of millions of dollars. At the National Guard armory, our voices echoing overhead, I asked our first sergeant why the farmers didn't just let the chickens freeze and then sell them as prefrozen, but he did not share my mirth.

"Go grab your gear," he said. "Uniform, rucksack, sleeping bag, cot if you have one. You might want to grab your gas mask, too."

None of us knew why he mentioned gas masks, but we drove home along the ice-slick roads to get our gear. In the living room, my mother was pacing back and forth.

"What is it?" she said. She lit another cigarette before she finished the first.

"Operation Save the Chickens," I told her. She looked at me blankly, so I explained what the first sergeant had told us—that the power was out and all the chicken houses across the countryside had no heat. The chickens would freeze to death, and we had been called to save them.

"Chickens," she said.

"Chickens," I told her.

"You're not going to war?"

"Not unless a chicken attacks me."

She hugged me hard enough to hurt. She smelled like smoke and love. Years later it would occur to me the code word should have been "Roaring Chicken" instead of "Roaring Bull."

Perhaps we simply wanted to pay the chickens back.

In the first Gulf War, with the threat of Hussein's chemical weapons and a severely slashed budget for the detection of them, the U.S. military enlisted chickens. The idea, like the canary in the coal mine, was that the chickens would detect chemical agents by dying, thus saving American lives, so "poultry chemical confirmation devices" were brought in. The official designation was Operation Kuwaiti Field Chicken, or KFC for short.

The Department of Defense used chickens again during the second Gulf War, in 2003. The plan this time was to place them in cages on top of caravans so troops moving into new areas would have an early detection system—if the chickens died, turn around.

Neither operation worked. In 2003, forty-one of the forty-three chickens sent to Iraq died shortly after arriving. In the first Gulf War, the chickens, standing sentry outside armed camps, froze to death in the cold desert night.

By the time I finished grabbing my gear, the ice was an inch deep on the roads. The sound it made on my windshield reminded me of fingernails tapping impatiently for me to get on with my life. I was, for a few more months, still considering a career in the military, but only because I had no other ideas. I was majoring in history at the time, and all the history classes I had taken only taught me that we make the same mistakes again and again. The present always circles back to the past while we're waiting for the future to get here.

At the armory, a long line of Humvees stood idling, ice falling like sparks in the red taillights. From our storage building, men were loading diesel generators into the backs of the Humvees, their voices broken by the fall of ice.

When the Humvees were loaded, First Sergeant Thomas called us to attention again and began laying out the plan: In pairs, we would be issued a Humvee with a generator. We'd be given directions to a farm and, once there, would hook up the generator to the chicken house and warm it enough to keep the chickens from freezing to death. Then we'd move to the next house, circling back through the night if need be.

I was paired with James Brighton, a guy my age who would end up in Antarctica years later. I suppose now he had a predilection for ice, but at the time I was disappointed Nikky Irby had not arrived so I could be paired with her, since the first sergeant had told us we might be out for weeks. He said to stay warm. He said to sleep when we could, and I was thinking of sleeping with Irby when someone asked where we would sleep. The ice was still falling; it would fall all that night and into the next day.

"Wherever you can," the first sergeant said.

By the time we left it was after midnight. I was already tired. For days my friends and I had been drinking too much, shooting pool, trying to convince ourselves there was a reason to go back to school. The temperature had dropped into the teens, and the ice slanted sideways in the headlights. The Humvee rattled and clanged as we drove, and the warm air from the heater stunk of diesel. I closed my eyes, thinking of bed.

It took us an hour to get to the first farm, though it was less than twenty miles away. The trees along the sides of the road were broken. In the light of morning we'd see snapped limbs everywhere, like some cataclysm had occurred in the night while we were trying to warm ourselves.

At the farm, a man with chapped hands and face met us in his driveway. He'd been checking the temperature in his chicken houses, waiting for us to arrive.

"I've already lost a few," he said, shaking our hands. Later I would learn he was responsible for the loss of chickens—every one that died was less money for him.

With the farmer directing us, James pulled the Hummer as close as he could to the first chicken house. We ran a long cord to the power supply. The farmer, whose name I've long forgotten, hooked it in, and a minute later we heard the heat come on.

The chickens, who seemed stunned in the cold—we could see our breath even inside the houses—circled each heat source. These were chicks, newly arrived. The farmer got a new batch every six weeks or so, grew them until they were big enough to fry, then shipped them out. He'd spend a few days cleaning out the houses—mucking the fouled sawdust and disposing of any dead chickens—and then more would come in. On summer days in Arkansas, we saw trucks full of small chicks or big fryers or sometimes chicken guts from the processing plants. The smell of manure hung over farm fields because many farmers laced them with fertilizer, and my friends and I were always saying the chicken crossed the road to get the fuck out of Arkansas. Years ago, the state of Oklahoma sued Arkansas for nonpoint water pollution, meaning the chemicals and waste from chicken houses got into the groundwater supply and poisoned Oklahoma wells. The chickens in Arkansas produce the waste equivalent of 9 million humans. The population of the state is 3 million.

All this is to say we stood there not talking while the heat climbed. In half an hour our breath no longer fogged before us, and a half hour after that we unzipped our heavy coats. The farmer's face was still red. His wife brought coffee she'd made over the fireplace, and we stood sipping as the farmer eyed the temperature gauge. Every few minutes he'd walk through the chicks to keep them moving.

"They're coming around," he'd say. "I can't tell you how glad I am you came."

— — — — — — — — — — —

We ran the generator to the first house for about two hours. It had gotten to be three in the morning. I got my cot from the Hummer and set it up in a far corner, and James and I took turns sleeping. Every so often I'd slip to sleep and wake with a jolt. The chickens crowded around the heat reminded me of humans, pecking at each other, jostling for space, trying to stay warm at someone else's expense. It didn't occur to me then that we are animals, and when what we have is taken away, we often revert to that animal nature.

Or so I'll say now. The truth is, I'm not sure what I thought that long night. I only remember that everything hurt. That I wondered why the Arkansas National Guard would spend state money to help a giant corporation. I suppose I could argue we were helping independent farmers, but at the time, in the cold, I thought about the protesters before Desert Shield became Desert Storm, chanting "no blood for oil" in the streets of Seattle. At the time I had thought them disrespectful of the men and women who were fighting for our freedom but later wondered if there was any truth to their chants. I wondered what freedom we were fighting for. As a history major, the more I studied war, the more I knew how corrupt we can become when we let greed control us. Those who argue the Civil War had nothing to do with slavery never took an economics class. The same with the War of 1812, the Barbary Wars, the Japanese expansion into the Pacific that brought about America's entry into World War II. In 1961, Eisenhower warned us of the military-industrial complex, which led me to ponder, while trying to sleep, about the chicken-industrial complex and what powers it wielded.

Around 4 a.m. we moved to the second house and repeated the process. More chicks were dead here, their small yellow bodies already turning stiff. The farmer scooped them up with a shovel and tossed them into a pit. Peering down into it at the dead bodies as the first gray wash of dawn shaped the far horizon, I imagined myself, much older, wandering the meat aisle at the local market, remembering.

By the time we made it to the third and then fourth house, around nine the next morning, there were chickens dead everywhere. The farmer came and went with his shovel and the pile in the pit grew. In the gray morning, the ice still fell on the roofs of the houses, and by the time we had warmed the fourth house, chickens were freezing again in the first.

At some point, seeing us shiver through the cold, the farmer brought out a little kerosene heater for us to put by our cot. It smoked and stunk and I thought it might catch the sawdust on fire, but let me say how far a small bit of comfort can go. As can kindness. In the moments we stood waiting for the heat to come on, the farmer told us how long he'd been trying to hold on to his land. Cattle prices had dropped years before, so he had switched to chickens, as many farmers in Arkansas had. And there was good money to be made, he said, only the profit margins were small. We would hear this story at every house we went to. "This may break me," these men would say, almost all of them in their fifties or sixties, which seemed incredibly old to me then, for men to be working through such sad weather without the advantage of young bodies. Most of them were at least a little overweight. They wore the red hands and weathered faces of men who work outside, and they carried with them the stoicism that comes from being at the mercy of the weather and other forces beyond their control.

A brief history of my family and Arkansas National Guard deployment:

In 1951, my grandfather's National Guard unit was deployed to Korea, where he worked in a hospital in Pusan. In a letter he wrote to his brother in pencil that has faded in the sixty years since, he says he wishes they could go fishing together and that he misses my mother, who was an infant at the time.

In 1957, the Arkansas National Guard was activated by Governor Orville Faubus and then federalized by Dwight D. Eisenhower. They were sent to Little Rock Central High School to protect nine African Americans integrating the school. My stepfather, who had lied about his age to join the guard and was barely older than the students at the school, was activated.

In 1968, my father's National Guard unit was activated after a tornado hit the neighboring town of Greenwood. For close to twenty-four hours he patrolled the ruins for looters. He had a weapon but no bullets.

And in 1993, I saved the lives of hundreds of thousands of chickens, which, translated, means I saved the chicken-industrial complex millions of dollars.

——— ——— ——— ——— ——— ——— ——— ——— ——— ——— ———

Despite being surrounded by chickens that would one day end up on someone's table, dipped twice in flour and fried to a crisp golden brown, all we had to eat were MREs issued to us at the armory. MREs, or meals ready to eat, are packaged in plastic and taste like sawdust. Many of them come with a small bottle of hot sauce, so they taste like sawdust with hot sauce, which is slightly more acceptable but not much. The first few days, most of the stores were closed so we could not stop to buy a bag of chips or a candy bar or those hot dogs that grow crusty and hard after all day in the warmer but still taste better than MREs.

And since both James and I carried all the hungers of the young within us, we talked constantly about food. Late at night, trying to sleep in the Humvee or on a cot inside the chicken house, we told each other of hamburgers and bacon, of breakfast sausage, of eggs, of all the pork rinds and beef jerky in the world. I did not know then how much meat we consume in our constant hunger, or how hard on our ecosystems things like nonpoint source pollution and methane gas from animal waste are. Nor did I know that the production of meat in our country uses more water than a trillion short showers, that the cattle industry contributes as much to climate change as all the cars we own, that a vast majority of agricultural land use is for raising livestock and not for growing the grain that feeds them.

So late one night, our stomachs rumbling like approaching airplanes, James and I came up with a plan to kill a chicken and cook it. We would wait until the farmer went to sleep and then catch and cut one's throat. We'd build a fire and put a spit over the fire and roast it like those guys in *All Quiet on the Western*

Front with that turkey or whatever it was, and we'd go to sleep full for once, if not clean.

But for whatever reason, we never got around to the killing. The farmer never slept long enough or we were too busy or we had spent too much time with the little chicks to eat them. So we stayed hungry, eating our cold MREs, until one evening the farmer's wife brought us sandwiches that we ate with our dirty hands like starving men.

— — — — — — — — — — —

The farmer's power came back on after we'd been there for two days. His wife brought us coffee once again and we stood in the cold with the warm cups in our hands, amazed at such small feelings. We had unhooked the generator and loaded it back in the Humvee and the farmer stood looking off at something we couldn't see. He offered his hand and we shook all around, and James and I climbed in the Humvee and drove back to the armory.

The power was back on in town and I thought we were through, but as soon as we pulled in, the first sergeant gave us the address of another house. I could not tell him—as a soldier, as a small boy who wanted to be a man—that I needed a hot shower and hot food and a warm bed. I needed to go home.

Instead, we climbed back in the Humvee and went higher into the hills, where the power was still out. Here trees had fallen under the weight of their own encasement. The hillsides glistened in the gray afternoon, and it seemed there was so much ice in the world even the mountains might collapse.

A farmer who seemed identical to the first met us in the driveway. I wondered how he had any chickens left alive after three days of freezing weather, but these were turkey houses. I do not know if turkeys are made of stronger stuff, if their bigger bodies offer them more protection from natural disasters such as ice falling unceasingly, or if the power had stayed on longer here.

What I know is that we were almost knocked out when we went inside the first house. The turkeys were full-grown, only a few days before they were to ship out. They filled the house with feathers, ten or twenty thousand of them gobbling in what seemed anger or discomfort. They had fouled the sawdust floor with shit so the whole house reeked of ammonia or smelling salts held under our noses to wake us up after a faint or fistfight.

"It's a little tough to get used to," the farmer said, and I felt the world spin around me. I went outside and breathed deep in the cold. Since the Gulf War I had wondered about myself as a soldier, if I had the fortitude to fight, and here I was scared of the smell of shit. I did not think I could stay in such a place, with the fumes of ammonia rising around me. But soldiers are supposed to be made of sterner stuff, so James and I dug through our gear and put on our gas masks. Later it would occur to me that despite all the talk of chemical warfare during Desert Storm, we'd been gassed here, in America, by turkeys.

— — — — — — — — — — —

That night was the coldest yet. The clouds had finally cleared, and in the powerless dark we could see them flung across the sky so bright I wanted to cry. We had to sleep at different times because someone had to be awake to keep the generator running, and it was hard to breathe in my gas mask, so when it was my turn to watch I would wander outside and stand under the stars and try to draw air. I was bone-tired, depressed, wondering, as all of us are, about our place here on earth, so to get through the long watches I pretended we were at war. That this was a brief respite before the bullets and bombs, before the world came crashing down around us. Like too many young men I invented heroic deeds—storming machine-gun nests, shooting down a suicide bomber, saving young children in the streets. I did not imagine guarding chickens.

I did imagine that we had deserted. The war was too long and we didn't know what we were fighting for, so we deserted and hid here, among the other chickens. Soon someone would come looking for us and we would be found and hanged. Before they hanged us, we would say we could not die for a cause we didn't believe in, although everyone who was on hand to see us hang would know we were just cowards.

I also wondered what would happen if I didn't go back to college. If I just threw on a backpack and set out on the road. I had already dropped out once, right after the Gulf War, after weeks of watching it on TV. There seemed no reason to go to class afterward. At any moment, another war would kick up and this time I'd be sent, and why worry about the future when there might not be one. I wondered if we would be called again to save the chickens or some other private industry. I wondered if that was why we went to the Gulf, and there in the dark it seemed certain that the war had never been about freedom but about protecting American interests in oil. The chickens all around me proved it.

As the night grew later, I wished that we had alcohol stashed away somewhere so I could get drunk and forget. That there was food here that didn't come from plastic or shit on its own floor. That the world didn't stink of decomposition, that we didn't send men to fight in the interests of money, that we weren't shitting all over the world in which we lived.

——— ——— ——— ——— ——— ——— ——— ——— ——— ———

There were more chicken and turkey houses, more farmers and MREs and long dark nights, but they all run together at this point. We were operating on too little sleep and too little food, and the whole time seems now one long scene of boredom and chicken shit and despair.

We spent two weeks working in the hills of Arkansas, saving the lives of chickens and (perhaps) farmers. As the power came back on in stages, we'd move on to the next house, always higher into the hills, farther away from the small towns that make up the region, deeper into economically depressed areas where farmers had to make tough choices if they wanted to keep their land. We heard stories of banks foreclosing on surrounding farms. Of the giant conglomerates forcing farmers to constantly upgrade their facilities or risk losing contracts. Of questionable business practices by the parent companies, and though I cannot verify the truth of those claims, the men I met were barely hanging on—we could see that in their run-down houses, their old farm trucks, their slumped shoulders, their gratitude that we had saved them, and I came to know they meant that we saved them from economic ruin, which might be, in this country, the same thing as saving their lives.

When we packed up at the last house, I came home. I slept for two days. I went back to college. I dropped out again. I left the military and got married and had kids and waited for another war to begin, knowing there was always another war waiting.

It was the only time I ever deployed, but not long before I left the military forever, my unit went to Fort Hood, Texas, for the weekend to fire missiles. This was the same base where Nidal Hasan, a U.S. Army major and psychiatrist, would fatally shoot thirteen people and injure thirty others and not far away from where sniper Chris Kyle would be shot and killed by a mentally disturbed former marine.

For years, my National Guard unit had not been deemed ready for active duty. Since shortly after the Korean War, it had been an evacuation hospital, and during a reorganization effort following the end of the Cold War, it had been converted to air defense artillery.

This was to be our qualification, our announcement that we were ready for war. Politicians from the state of Arkansas had flown down to witness the event. Generals and colonels and sergeants major were on hand as well as, I believe, representatives from the missile company.

Our first sergeant wanted all the men my age out of the way, so he had told us the night before we could drink in the barracks. Two dozen of us, the youngest kids, the ones who would work the front lines if we ever went to war, the ones who had, mostly, saved the chickens and stood at attention at the graves of soldiers who had died in Vietnam, got so stinking drunk that the next day our heads hurt so badly we could hardly move.

We loaded a bus before first light and drove an hour out to the firing range, a long expanse of scrub brush in the Texas countryside. Most of us were still hurting, so in a move we saw at the time as magnanimous, our first sergeant said we could sleep it off in the scrub brush as long as we stayed out of sight.

The artillery had been set up down in a little valley. On the top of the hill, a platform had been erected for the representatives and senators. From behind us, a large rocket, shaped like a ship, would be fired, and from down on the valley floor our missiles would shoot it out of the sky while the visiting dignitaries watched.

The rest of us slept in the scrub brush, too hurt to care. As the sun moved our shade, we crawled farther into the brush, and when the first missile fired we didn't see it. I heard later there was an explosion, and the politicians cheered and the missiles streaked the sky like a sign of coming war, but I didn't know. I had put in my earplugs so I wouldn't hear anything. I kept crawling deeper into the brush to block out the sun. As if I didn't want to see, like a man, or bird, with his head in the sand.

THIS IS MY RIFLE

A few months after I moved to North Carolina, I was sitting on a porch with a half dozen other people, drinking and talking about writing, movies, books we loved. It was October, cool enough to be pleasant, and the drinks tasted fine and a light wind stirred the falling leaves. I had just started graduate school, and though I didn't know any of the people very well then, they were weird and funny and smart and I was in a new city with a new life stretching out in front of me, when four men wearing ski masks and carrying pistols ran up onto the porch.

It was around eleven o'clock. The table was littered with empty beer cans and drink glasses and ashtrays overflowing with cigarette butts. I sat in a cheap plastic chair. Two people sat in the porch swing. Another couple stood by the door, another on a bar stool we had dragged outside, another in a recliner salvaged from the curbside on trash pickup day. When the men ran up the porch stairs, we all froze. I could see the guns gleaming in the porch light. Through the open window came the sound of a radio.

"Give me your fucking money," one of them said.

Two of the men stood by the porch steps, heads swiveling from the street to us and back. They held their guns by their sides. The other two moved among us, like you've seen on any number of TV shows or movies, taking watches and wallets.

But we were grad students, and none of us wore expensive watches or rings or necklaces. None of us carried cash.

By the time one of the men made it to me, he was getting angry. He had gotten no money from any of us. I could see his eyes through his ski mask. His knuckles were white where they held the gun.

He pressed the gun hard enough into my stomach I could feel the coldness of the steel.

"Give me your fucking money," he said.

My wallet was in my front pocket, my jacket covering it. I'd had a few drinks and the air was cool and I was in a new city and the whole thing seemed surreal, so I told him I didn't have any money. I even shrugged casually as I said it. I thought they would simply run off, but by this point he was too angry to give up. He moved the gun from my stomach to my neck. His fingernails were clean, I noticed. Strange what you notice at a time like that. One of the others said, "Let's go," but he shook his head slightly, just a twitch really, then pushed the barrel of the gun into my neck hard enough my head moved. He cocked the hammer.

"You got any money now, motherfucker?" he said.

— — — — — — — — — —

I do not know whether this was a beginning or an ending. In the years since I had left the military, I had begun to write and to question, through my work, my time in the service, the things I had done as a soldier, and the things American soldiers did on foreign soil. I wondered what the word "freedom" meant, and I was worried about, among other things, the quintessentially American idea that guns make us safer, whether we're aiming them at enemies or only carrying them around in case we need them.

I had also begun to question what I would have done if I had seen Desert Storm. If I had stayed in the military afterward and been sent to Afghanistan. I wondered what I would have done if a man raised his rifle and aimed it toward me, if rockets rained down out of the sky, if bombs and bullets were always exploding in the air around us. The night with the gun in my neck was little more than a month after 9/11 and that feeling of hopelessness we all had when the towers came down. The first troops had arrived in Afghanistan, and already our State Department was turning its eye to Iraq and our interests there. I still knew soldiers, men who would be shipped overseas, and I still woke some nights wondering if I would be among them.

I do not know, had I been sent to war, if I would have stood and returned fire, or if I would have huddled in a corner hoping it all went away. I wonder what I would have done seeing children huddled in a corner, hoping it all went away. I do not like this line of questioning, nor do I like the one that follows, the wondering if it ever just all goes away. What I mean is: is there an actual end or only more beginnings?

— — — — — — — — — — —

I got my first gun for my twelfth birthday, a bolt-action .410 with a blonde stock. It held three shells. It had belonged to my grandfather, who fought in World War II and Korea, and that fall I walked through the woods behind my house with it every afternoon as the dark came early and the leaves left the trees.

When I was seventeen, I joined the military. When we qualified with our M16s, I hit thirty-five out of forty targets, one short of expert. In the second half of my military training, I learned to disassemble and reassemble the M16, the M60, the M249 Squad Automatic Weapon, the M203 grenade launcher, the 9mm, and the .50-caliber machine gun as well as fire all of them. I've fired thousands of rounds in the military and thousands more with hunting rifles and pistols, and that October night I was as prepared as any man could ever be, short of a soldier or police officer who trains for just such occasions.

— — — — — — — — — — —

Some nights I dream about the gun. The cold steel. The gleam in the porch light. There is no one standing over me. The gun is simply there. Soon the trigger will pull. There will come a brief flash, then the acrid smell of smoke, though I do not know if I will be alive to smell it, to see the flash, to hear the report.

In Tobias Wolff's short story "Bullet in the Brain," the main character, Anders, does not hear the bullet, or smell the smoke, or feel it penetrate his flesh. It carves a furrow into his forehead, but he is not there to know. He is remembering a long-lost Saturday afternoon during the heat of summer. A baseball game. A boy chanting in right field. He is remembering the power of words.

Had the gun fired when it was pressed against my neck, my last words would have been "I don't have any money."

The last word I would have heard was "motherfucker."

In the dream, I think that I do not want "motherfucker" to be the last thing I ever hear. Nor do I want there to be a last thing.

— — — — — — — — — — —

I am writing this a few days after twenty-six people, twenty of them children, were killed at Sandy Hook Elementary School in Connecticut. Six months after a gunman walked into a movie theater in Aurora, Colorado, and opened fire with an assault rifle. Five years after thirty-two people were killed at Virginia Tech, which is not very far away, geographically or metaphorically, from where I teach at a small liberal arts college. Thirteen years after Columbine, eleven after 9/11 and the invasion of Afghanistan.

I keep thinking of that classroom. My wife teaches kindergarten, and I see her room, which I have visited many times. I see her children, some of whom, from previous years, are stored on digital photos on my computer and often pop up when the screensaver switches on. The gunman would have walked through a door with a handwritten sign on it that says "Welcome to Mrs. Crenshaw's Kindergarten Class!!!" My wife would have been standing at the board or sitting at her desk. The children would have been coloring, or learning to form letters, or sitting in a circle on the carpet listening to my wife read.

She would have been the first to see him. To see the rifle raised. To see the fire shoot—I imagine this in slow motion—from the barrel as the bullets began to fly. She would have been the first one shot, and the last thing she saw would have been the bodies of her students falling beside her, their little shirts and dresses blooming now with blood, their mouths trying to form words but finding only screams, or nothing. I imagine seeing that would have been hard, although perhaps not as hard as the phone calls some parents would get later in the day. To learn that, only a single moment before it all began and everything ended—everything in your entire world—your children had been practicing their *R*s, or drawing pictures of winter, or listening to my wife's voice as she read to them about a snowy day as I have heard her read to my daughters hundreds of times.

— — — — — — — — — — —

In Flannery O'Connor's short story "A Good Man Is Hard to Find," the Misfit says the grandmother "would have been a good woman if it had been somebody there to shoot her every minute of her life," but while the gun was in my neck that night, I only thought of being powerless, how it feels an awful lot like being alone, and small, and scared.

— — — — — — — — — — —

I think about the noise the gun must have made in that classroom. I think about the broken glass, the pools of blood. The children with their eyes closed as they were led out. The phone calls, cells vibrating in pockets, rattling against floors where children lay facedown.

Outside, the sun slanted toward winter. Leaves went rattling along the sidewalk. The rest of us were going to work or drinking coffee at a window, steam from the cup condensing on the glass. My daughters had climbed on buses only an hour before, were sitting in classrooms much like that one. I was sitting at my computer as I do every morning, trying to make some sense of the world with the words I write. That morning, I kept thinking about the bus pulling away. That classroom. The way my wife looks when I visit unannounced and stand outside her room looking through the little window in the door. She doesn't see me, but I watch her with her children.

Like most of us, I felt something break. Like most of us, I will spend days or years or forever trying to understand what it was. That morning, I kept writing the same lines again and again:

What is wrong with us? What in the world is wrong with us?

— — — — — — — — — — —

I keep coming back to the gun in my neck. It's the only thing I can relate to, the powerlessness I felt, and I wonder now how the fear of being powerless moves us in ways we might not admit.

I also imagine that men want to see themselves as strong. As protectors, whether of freedom or only a front porch, a few dollars in a wallet. As a child, I thought being a man meant having a mustache; as an adult, I see how often we act as protectors or predators, how much we fear being prey.

So I keep returning to that October night. Wind in the trees. Drinking and talking too loudly with writer friends about what most moved us in the world, about what we might change if only we can capture the words to unlock what most moves others.

The guy in the ski mask patted me down and found my wallet. He kept the gun to my neck as he dug it out of my pocket. He flipped it open, saw the money, and took the gun away.

The four of them ran off down the street. My friends and I looked at each other in disbelief, then called 911. In a few minutes the police arrived, guns drawn, but the men were gone.

Some nights I think that if I had had my own gun, I could have defended myself. I could have pulled it out and squeezed off a few rounds. The robbers would have shot back. The others on the porch would have dived for cover. If they had guns they could have started shooting too. The robbers would retreat from the porch, all of them firing. Perhaps a bullet would have gone across the street, broken a window, and the owner would have come out with his gun, firing back at us. The police, upon arriving, would not have known who were the good guys and who were the bad guys, and they would have started shooting as well, until all up and down the street, all over the city, all over the state, all over the world, people were firing at one another, and it would be easy to believe this is the way the world would end.

It wouldn't be anybody's fault, and there wouldn't be anything you could do about it.

RED DAWN

The first thing I ever wanted to be was a Jedi knight. I wanted a lightsaber that would make that whooshing sound and to be able to do front flips and backflips while fending off heavily breathing enemies in oddly shaped masks. I wanted to make hair dryers and fine china fly across the room at my brother when he wouldn't let me watch TV or at my stepfather when he made me do chores or, at the very least, to be able to do my chores with my Jedi powers.

When I learned that Jedi knights weren't real, I wanted to be a ninja, and when I found out you could actually become a ninja I wanted to move to Japan and join a ninja school, where, I was sure, I would run obstacle courses and practice sword fighting and underwater breathing and the ancient art of deception. I begged my mother to allow me to go, but for some reason she refused to take my request seriously. I tried to explain how I wanted to walk on water and catch arrows midair, to scale buildings using ninja claws and rappel back down on a rope I had hidden to make my escape after I assassinated the emperor. I wanted to hide in bushes and shoot blowgun darts at passing enemies, or throw metal sharpened into a star shape at them, or while retreating into the night, toss down a smoke bomb and disappear in a flash or throw those little spiky things over my shoulder, where they would stick into the soles of my pursuers' feet and cause them to hop around saying, "Ouch, ouch, those little spiky things really hurt."

My mother seemed to think this a passing phase, so to prove her wrong I began ordering throwing stars from the back of *Black Belt* and *Kung Fu* magazines. My best friend, Thomas, had also decided his life's work was to become a ninja, and on weekends we climbed trees and ran through the woods dressed in black—or dark blue when our ninja clothes were in the wash. When we weren't slinking through the backyards of nearby houses or scaling the elementary school building, we watched old B movies where ninjas infiltrated guarded compounds, taking out enemy soldiers one by one until only the baddest bad guy was left, or D movies where Mexican ninjas in sweatpants and ski toboggans swung nunchucks slowly around their heads and the dubbed voice said, "I keel you for honor and revenge and honor."

We began to stockpile weapons. After seeing Bruce Lee wield nunchucks to take out hordes of fat guys in *Game of Death*, we built two pairs with dowel rods and lengths of gilded chain normally used for hanging plants. When the handles began to fly off our homemade versions, we mail ordered nunchucks identical to those in the movie, and when my mother caught me slinging them around in the middle of the living room, right under the ceiling fan and right next to the glass coffee table and the TV, she agreed to enroll me in karate classes, most likely out of fear that without some form of guidance I would concuss myself.

After we started karate, Thomas and I spent hours, when we weren't sneaking through the neighborhood at night or watching *Revenge of the Ninja* or *Enter the Ninja* or *The Octagon*, fighting in my front yard. These fights often ended after a broken toe or a dislocated shoulder or a chipped tooth, but they seemed fun at the time. The idea was not to hurt each other but to become better fighters, although it escapes me now why we needed to become better fighters. I suppose we thought that, like Chuck Norris's character in *The Octagon*, we might suddenly find out a twin brother we didn't remember had started a school for evil ninjas and it was up to us to end it or that we would be asked to infiltrate a drug lord's hideout by entering his martial arts contest, and obviously we could not uncover a secret drug ring or end our evil twin's reign of terror without superior fighting skills.

The karate class also opened up a whole new world of weapons. We had a few throwing stars and nunchucks, but along the walls of our classroom were long staves called *bōs* and short staves called *jōs*. There were replica daggers and soft nunchucks we could beat each other with. There were *sais* and *juttes* and *tonfas* and *kama* and a few swords, both wooden and real, although our instructor had disappointingly forgotten to order smoke bombs and ninja claws and little spiky things.

We did not know at the time that the Russians had huge stockpiles of nuclear weapons and so did America. After seeing the movie *Red Dawn*, in which Soviet and Cuban soldiers parachute in to take over a small Colorado town, we decided nunchucks were as useless as the dialogue in martial arts movies. Ninjas were not the enemy—Russians were. And while nunchucks might work for taking out bad guys with sticks, they would never work against Kalashnikov-wielding comrades.

We both begged for guns for our birthdays and practiced by shooting tiny birds and small woodland creatures and occasionally feral cats. Besides the ability to kung fu fight and shoot enemy soldiers, we needed to learn to live off the land and to know our surroundings in case the Russians ever came. We would hide in the hills, feeding ourselves, and make guerilla attacks against these occupiers. Our families would suffer, but they would live free in their hearts knowing their children were out in the wilds, fighting to take the country back and occasionally shooting bears and pumas and squirrels.

We watched *Red Dawn* again and again. Also: *Godzilla* and *WarGames* and *Mechagodzilla* and *The Day After*, any movie where outside forces threatened us. I think now we were just kids, and bored. But perhaps we were like people everywhere, trying to find some meaning in our existence, and an outside threat gave us both meaning and existence. Fighting for humanity's survival would be the ultimate sacrifice, although we weren't actually planning on sacrificing anything. Our imaginations of how this might occur ended with the glorification of war, the hero's welcome, the emotional gristle of suffering rendered through a fake lens. Perhaps we didn't plan the whole thing out very well or think it all the way through.

We bought more guns. I bought a pistol my parents didn't know about. Some days I carried it to school tucked into my pants. I kept it under my bed and sometimes took it out at night while the moon fell in the window after I woke dreaming of Russians parachuting in, missiles flying across the world and arcing downward. They would land in a silent circle on a computer screen somewhere. We would hear nothing, only see a bright light at the very end. After that, the world would descend into chaos as the Russians invaded, and only those prepared for the coming battle would survive it.

Even after we grew older we spent a lot of time watching movies about the coming apocalypse. And ninjas. Occasionally we fought in the front yard and, some nights, crept through the neighborhood wearing black and pretending our neighbors were invading Russians, but both of us began to suspect *Red Dawn* and others movies like it were intellectually dishonest, preying on the cliché of the average American rising up to defend his homeland against outside forces, whether commie atheist socialist Russians or postapocalyptic cyborgs or aliens from outer space or evil ninjas bent on world domination. We suspected the movies depicted a world that didn't really exist except on the screen, or in the imagination, or in the fear of "others" that pervaded our country.

Then Gorbachev began his glasnost and perestroika business and the Cold War ended, along with any threat of invading Russians. Besides which, we decided, instead of an invasion of soldiers there would have been an invasion of missiles, and after such an invasion there would be no survivors except maybe a few monasteries of ninjas deep in the mountains of Japan who would then rule the world, until they assassinated one another because there was no one left to assassinate. Or the aliens would come in with superior technology. Or the cyborgs would rise up.

At seventeen, I joined the military and a few months later shipped to Basic Training. At the rifle range we shot at cut-outs of Russian soldiers. We tossed dummy grenades at more Russian cutouts and stabbed others with our bayonets. We traipsed through the woods carrying rifles, but it was nothing like what Thomas and I had imagined. It was too hot, and bugs swarmed everywhere, and there was always the threat of being gassed. I wrote to Thomas that the days were long and tiring and we mostly did push-ups, and even firing an M16 wasn't that much fun, lying on gravel in 100-degree heat. He was a year younger than me and considering joining the military as well.

"Don't," I wrote him. "Just don't."

I was in college when the Gulf War began. I cut pictures from the newspaper of soldiers leaving home, then landing on airfields in Saudi Arabia, disembarking in the swimming heat. Once the war began I collected pictures of night-vision lenses over Baghdad catching the bombs lighting the city and the tracer fire of antiaircraft batteries frozen in flight, Apache helicopters and A-10 Thunderbolts and multiple launch rocket systems firing skyward.

My roommate and I got drunk every night, and in the morning we'd say we wished we were there but were really too hurt to move. Eventually, we quit drinking. The war, like everything else, grew old, and we began to watch G.I. Joe or Transformers cartoons. Both dealt in war, but the animation proclaimed that it wasn't real, allowed us to indulge in the romantic notion that here was a war in which no one ever died.

And though no good ninja movies have been made in twenty years, it is now easy to find war coverage anywhere in the world, any time of day or night. The United States still has troops in Afghanistan and Iraq. We still have bases in Germany and Japan and Korea. Late at night the History Channel shows World War II in color, and the Military Channel recreates old battles, complete with eyewitness testimonies and expert opinion.

Ninja movies have been replaced by *Game of Thrones*. By *Rome* and *The Sopranos* and *The Walking Dead*, though I don't think anyone over the age of thirteen wants to take on Jaime Lannister or Titus Pullo in a sword fight. No one really wants to be Jason Bourne. Or the guy in *The Deer Hunter*. Or *Platoon* or *Full Metal Jacket* or *Saving Private Ryan* or *The Hurt Locker* or *All Quiet on the Western Front* or *Apocalypse Now*.

At some point you outgrow all that. You realize you never wanted to be a Jedi knight or a ninja, or you only wanted it with the strange emotions of childhood, the belief that what you see is real and the feelings the images stir inside you are as real as the images themselves. Sneaking through someone's backyard at night can get a person my age arrested. Infiltrating heavily guarded compounds means something bad is going to happen, whether the person doing the infiltrating is carrying a blowgun or a machine gun, and at some point you realize even if it is the baddest of the bad guys, no matter what he has done in this world, he is going to lose his life.

Those things don't turn out well even in movies. Be honest— you never wanted Russian paratroopers to land outside your high school in Colorado. You never wanted to flee to the mountains, to see family and friends killed. You never wanted to wake to the sound of bombs in the distance and fighters streaking overhead, machine guns rattling through the empty streets of the town where you live.

And at some point, you begin to wonder if people in other countries feel that way too.

NOTES ON A MASSACRE

"We tell ourselves stories in order to live," Joan Didion wrote in "The White Album," prefacing the time she began to distrust all the stories she had told herself, which she had allowed to continue unquestioned. To her princess caged in the consulate I would add the knight-errant performing valorous deeds, for surely this is the story we tell ourselves in order to soothe our troubled psyches when we hear of a massacre in Mosul or My Lai forty years after the fact. We are knights in shining armor, wielding sword and shield, one for power and the other protection, and we have been called to this quest. "This war is being waged for peace," we say, and "Only with aggression can we become passive." By building arms that destroy we are saving the world. Missile strikes are strategic and surgical, words that betray both common usage and common sense. These are fictions, contradicting ideas that only make sense if one applies a special brand of sightless logic. They are stories we repeat so often we hear them as truth.

Other stories we tell to keep our egos inflated. We are exceptional, because we live in an exceptional country that was made exceptional by our exceptionalness. Even God blesses us, for we ask Him to at the end of every speech. Our might is both right and righteous, so onward, Christian soldiers. At the end of Desert Storm, after a month of bombing and then a quick uncontested trek across the trackless waste, there were many among us who claimed we were looked upon by a just and caring God. To the cheering crowds lining the streets of Columbia, South Carolina, where I was serving in the army when the soldiers returned, we were indeed blessed.

So we think. Sometime after the end of the Gulf War, my story veered off track and I began to question, as Didion did, everything I had heard. The cheering crowds and celebratory parades ended with the summer, and we all settled into another season. It was in this quiet afterward that I began to deconstruct both story and image of the world and myself. I wanted to see if the princess was indeed caged in the consulate. If the pied piper can play his seductive flute and lead us out of the towns and cities we have inhabited into the undiscovered country, the uncomfortable concept that paradise is overbooked and heaven may not be real. We are no more exceptional than anyone else and certainly no more blessed. Twenty-five years later I have come to suspect our stories are only as real as the war that brings peace, but we hold on to them hard, because to do otherwise would cause the strings to unravel and the tapestry to fall. The center cannot hold.

I am writing about a time now in the early 90s, not long after the Berlin Wall fell and George Bush Sr. spoke about a thousand points of light and a kinder, gentler nation. I am writing about a war that was both popular and victorious, what we thought was an American win in the Middle East, though of course the war isn't over and may never be. But our fear of extremist acts begins and ends with one area of the world, and all the kidnappings and car bombings of the 70s and 80s were cleaned away by our quick victory in the Gulf. We stood on the cusp of a new decade, and the worries and tragedies of the last two had been pushed aside like the roads army engineers bulldozed through the desert.

When the war ended, we went back to our real lives. The troops returned home and we all waved our flags. I kept my hair cut short and covered my heart when "The Star-Spangled Banner" played from the loudspeakers at football games. For all outward appearances I was a normal, semiproductive member of society, but there seemed to be sand stuck in my throat, an irritation I couldn't quite kick. The knight's shield might claim protection but can also be used to smash in a face on the backswing. The princess may be perfectly happy where she is, her rescue unwanted. If God does have a plan, He could also have the benevolence to bless more than one country in the world.

What I mean to say is that there are stories circulating in our collective psyches unquestioned. Rapunzel lets down her hair, and we never bother to ask if it can bear the weight of the climber. We never wonder how the evil queen mistakes the heart of an animal for that of her stepdaughter, or if the kiss of the prince would really wake the woman struck down by the poisoned apple. Few people I knew ever questioned whether God really blessed our country above all others. Few wondered where all the missiles went or how many men watched them arcing downward in the last seconds of their lives.

Near the No Gun Ri rail bridge in South Korea in July 1950, the 7th Cavalry, U.S. Armed Forces, killed at least 163 Korean civilians and wounded at least 55 others. Many more were listed as missing. The South Korean government, in 2005, estimated that as many as 250 to 300 were killed.

The story reads like this, as far as it can be reconstructed over such time and distance: On July 26, the 8th Army, amid reports that North Korean guerilla troops were disguising themselves as civilians, ordered that all movement along the roads be stopped. No refugees were to cross battle lines at any time. Hundreds or thousands of them had been forced from their homes by advancing troops, but the movement, the order came, was to cease immediately.

One day before the decision, U.S. soldiers had removed hundreds of civilians from villages near the town of Yongdong in central South Korea and ordered them south along the main road. The next day these civilian refugees approached a railroad bridge near the village of No Gun Ri.

The 7th Cav, in fortified positions near the rail bridge, opened fire on the civilians. Most of them were women and children, screaming until their voices were forever silenced. Some pulled dead bodies around themselves for protection. Survivors of the attack said the stream ran red with blood. When night fell, the trapped refugees tried to crawl to safety. Many of them were shot.

"The American soldiers played with our lives like boys playing with flies," said Chun Choon-ja, a twelve-year-old girl at the time. One soldier said, as the fear and confusion of battle came over them all, "The hell with those people. Let's get rid of them." They didn't know if the refugees were North or South Koreans, civilians or soldiers. The American soldiers—green recruits in many instances, young kids so scared some of them threw down their rifles and fled at reports of an approaching enemy—had only been in-country a couple of days and didn't know the Koreans from "a load of coal," so they shot them all to make themselves safe.

"On summer nights when the breeze is blowing, I can still hear their cries, the little kids screaming," one soldier said. A Korean survivor, who was sixteen at the time of the attack, said she can still hear the moans of women dying in a pool of blood. "Children cried and clung to their dead mothers."

This story lay silent for twenty-two years before I was born and another twenty-five after that. As the 38th parallel was drawn and the Cold War grew colder still. As the French fell to the communists at Dien Bien Phu and more American troops flew to Southeast Asia. As the Vietcong soldier was shot in the head on the nightly news. As Cronkite pronounced the war unwinnable and Nixon was toppled from power. As we held our hands over our hearts every morning all through elementary school. As the bicentennial came and went. As troops invaded Grenada and the air force lobbed missiles at Libya and 241 marines died in Lebanon. As the Soviet Union crumbled and the Berlin Wall came down and we heard about all these things on the news every night. As Hussein invaded Kuwait. As the U.S.-led coalition invaded Iraq. As the bombs began to fall.

In 1998, after reading an account of the attack by one of the survivors, three AP reporters began investigating. Their story was published in 1999. In 2000, railroad workers patched over the bullet holes in the concrete.

—— —— —— —— —— —— —— —— —— —— ——

What does one do with a story like this? There are, to be fair, conflicting accounts. Some sources make the numbers smaller. Some say it was an unfortunate accident, that these things happen in war. They shake their heads and stare at the ground until the uncomfortable moment passes. Mistakes were made. A full investigation is being launched.

In the meantime, we must learn to live with the image of American soldiers shooting unarmed civilians. A stream running red as biblical prophecy. With the recounting of a woman whose five-year-old son and two-year-old daughter died in the darkness beneath that bridge with American bullets in their bodies. We tell ourselves stories in order to live, though sometimes we turn away from them to keep from questioning what we've always been taught.

—— —— —— —— —— —— —— —— —— —— ——

We begin with stories. When your mother was pregnant. The night you were born. When you were teething. Before you could walk. That house, there. On that tree-lined street. The winter of '16 or fall of '48 or the summer of '72.

We move from our origins into fantasy worlds. The night Max made mischief of the worst kind and a forest grew in his room. Goodnight, comb and brush and bowl full of mush, goodnight, old lady whispering hush. We are read stories of giving trees and green eggs and hungry caterpillars. We read of talking pigs and spiders that can spell. Of wind in the willows and holes in the ground in which there lived a hobbit.

In elementary school we move to history, but our subjects still hold the flavor of story. "In 1492," we all recite, "Columbus sailed the ocean blue," and certainly Columbus did sail and certainly he was on an ocean. We are told that he "miscalculated" distance, and in the 70s it even might have been stated somewhere in the curricula that it was Columbus who proved the earth was not flat. Later we learn this is not the truth. We also learn that along with "discovering" a land that had been populated with people for somewhere around ten thousand years, Columbus was not even the first European to "discover" it, yet we accept this as part of the learning process, that we are not told the entire story at a certain age or are told fictionalized versions (the lost colony of Roanoke, for instance, or Thanksgiving).

We are not told in first grade about the slaughter and enslavement of Indigenous peoples that Columbus oversaw. We do not learn of the diseases the Europeans contaminated the Natives with, how they had no immunity to the plague or measles or smallpox and died by the millions. We learn that the first settlers on Plymouth Rock were welcomed by the Indians, but the truth is these diseases had wiped out the Native population; the Pilgrims settled at Plymouth Rock because the fields were already planted, the forests cleared, and the Natives were all dead.

Our atrocities are most often removed from high school history. We learn of Tutankhamun and Amenhotep but not My Lai. Custer's last stand but never No Gun Ri. Neither Pizarro's march to the Pacific nor Cortes's conquering of Tenochtitlan ever make much more than a footnote, one that, from what I remember, focuses more on the superior firepower of the Spanish than their failure to see the Incans or Aztecs as human beings, as if it were their fault for not having enough fortitude to fight against steel and storm.

What the history books fail to tell us is that they are written by those who would censor history, as several states are now pushing to do, eliding the unsavory act of slavery and replacing that portion of our past with the more upbeat idea of American exceptionalism. Any stories that might make us question the intent or integrity of our founding fathers are now spun delicately into threads we would have to unravel elsewhere to find truth, buried as it is under an idea promoting our country's creation and not the facts surrounding that idea. America may be exceptional, but it is only because we have the opportunity to learn from our mistakes, which cannot happen if we fictionalize the past more than it already has been.

But to the victor go the spoils, or, in this case, the saturation and obfuscation of fact. Or the general omission thereof. As if it never happened or is now too difficult to deal with and is best left alone, residing still in the distant past, ever uncovered.

——— ——— ——— ——— ——— ——— ——— ——— ——— ———

It's no coincidence that when I began to assemble such thoughts was around the time I began to read heavily. I didn't read Orwell or Didion then—those came later—but Herbert and Tolkien. This was not reading for enlightenment but escape, a way of looking for a world that wasn't there.

I didn't know at the time that Tolkien had served in World War I, that the orcs catapulting human heads over the walls of Minas Tirith symbolized the horrors he saw in the trenches, or that Leto's visions in the later *Dune* books were of a way for humankind to expand across the universe so that we might

become so scattered and populated we can keep from destroying ourselves. I didn't know that both Tolkien and Herbert (and
Bradbury and Asimov and Clarke) feared the dangers of indus-
trialization and technology enough to incorporate it into their
work, using story as a frame to warn of unlimited wealth, the
corrupting influence of unending armies, and machines that
can think.

What I thought of instead were oil fires burning under a
night sky where the star of Bethlehem had once shone. Of
forces massed near the Plains of Megiddo. Of another book
that recounts the end of the world in bloody battle and that there
are people on this planet who are looking forward to that end.
How prophecy can self-fulfill. How stories are metaphor and
how sometimes we believe the metaphor to be real.

I was only beginning to believe then that sometimes the
metaphor actually is real. I was studying history at the time,
and economics, none of which made sense except in light of the
books I was reading. Our economics professor never mentioned
the term "oligarchy," but I could see it in the way the dragon
guarded the treasure or the sandworms guarded the spice. The
dwarves, cast out from their earnings beneath their mountain
home, come to reclaim their treasure from the tyrant who has
benefitted from their hard work. The spice must flow, the emperor says in *Dune*, then uses its exchange as a means for murder, all of which made sense in our modern economy, where
the dragon does guard the treasure. He has stolen away all the
wealth. He lies sleeping now beneath the mountain, upon his
pile of gold.

— — — — — — — — — — — —

Sometime before the invasions of Iraq and Afghanistan; before 9/11; before the Oklahoma City bombing; before Grenada
and the van bomb in Beirut; before the Soviet Union's newly
installed radar detected five American Minuteman missiles
and so began a launch sequence that would have destroyed

the world had it not been stopped by a young captain who did not trust the new technology; sometime before My Lai, where 500 Vietnamese civilians were murdered by American troops; sometime before Robert Kennedy was shot, before the Cuban Missile Crisis, before the Bay of Pigs, before Sputnik and the space race, before No Gun Ri and the Battle of Chosin Reservoir; before Hiroshima and Nagasaki, before Dresden and D-day, before Midway and Iwo Jima and Pearl Harbor; before all the conflicts of the nineteenth century that led us to modern warfare with tanks and airplanes and machine guns and nerve gas; before the annihilation of native tribes all over the world; before the systematic slaughter of African countries in the cause of colonialism; before the invention of gunpowder; before the Inquisition, before the Black Plague, before the Crusades; before the fall of Rome; before the pyramids, before papyrus, before cuneiform and hieroglyphics or any way to keep the history of the written word, records tell the story that man had a tendency to murder.

In an underground cavern called Sima de los Huesos, or "Pit of Bones," in northern Spain, paleontologists found, among the many bones buried for half a million years, a skull wearing two gaping wounds in its forehead. The two holes are nearly identical in size and shape, meaning they were made by the same weapon, most likely a stone axe. Meaning that whoever struck, struck twice. Meaning that almost before man learned to walk upright, he learned to kill, then hide what he had done.

——— —— — —— — —— — —— — —— ——

In Willa Cather's novel *My Ántonia*, the Russian Pavel tells this story on his deathbed:

When they were much younger, he and his brother Peter, along with others of their isolated Russian village, attended a wedding deep in the woods. Late in the night, after much feasting and toasting and proclamations of long life, the marriage party started back to the village in sleighs over the deep snow.

In the cold and dark they heard the howl of wolves and soon saw yellow eyes tracking them through the night. They urged the horses to more speed, but the horses floundered. The wolves snapped at the hooves of the horses in the last sleigh and fouled the reins. The sleigh went down in the snow and the wolves closed in, breaking bone and rending flesh. The screams, it seems to me now, would echo forever into that long night.

Soon more wolves took the next sleigh and the one after that. I don't remember how many there were, only that eventually there was only one sleigh left, driven by the Russian brothers and carrying the bride and groom. The wolves were all around. The horses grew terrified. The Russian brothers grew terrified as well, and in the last moment before the wolves took them down, the brothers turned and lifted the bride and groom from the sleigh and threw them to the wolves.

The moral of that story is easy, I thought, when I first read it in college. Not so, now. The man who moralizes will say he would never do such a thing. I say we do it every day.

In 1990, during the Gulf War, which was code-named Operation Desert Storm, as if a new wind were blowing through the Middle East, we first heard of smart bombs and surgical strikes. Of the Apache helicopter and the A-10 Thunderbolt and FLIR tracking and night-vision lenses. Of the Tomahawk cruise missile and satellite imaging. War became a commodity, one beamed into our homes from Baghdad. It gave rise to the twenty-four-hour news network, and the network advertised it as a thing to be valued.

Among the coverage were tutorials on all those things I mentioned before. Wolf Blitzer told us how Tomahawks would be used to take out radio stations but leave orphanages untouched.

How the Apache's FLIR cameras would destroy the Republican Guard's tanks, how an amphibious landing would draw the more dangerous troops toward the coast. Colonels and majors and major generals explained how the war would be won and when the war started explained how we were winning, how we had carefully controlled the destruction, had ripped apart Iraq's infrastructure and destroyed their communications capability and rendered them as blind as Saul on the road to Damascus. Our superior firepower was stressed. Our ability to inflict few civilian casualties was commended.

In one interview after the war, Gen. Norman Schwarzkopf plays a video clip of a farm truck rattling slowly across a bridge hovering in the cross hairs of a B-2 bomber. The general prefaces the action by saying, "Here is the luckiest man in Iraq," and surely enough the man seems quite lucky, for moments after the truck disappears from the scene, the bridge explodes when the missile strikes. The gathered press laugh because destruction, of course, is the victor's spoil, and laughter, the best medicine.

— — — — — — — — — — —

Over 2,500 years, church scholars culled portions of the Bible because of conflicting ideas or contradictory dogma or simply because they did not believe the Apocrypha carried God's word. Perhaps these parts contained ambiguous moral lessons that needed to be carefully controlled. Or stories true believers might not need to hear, as if the gospel truth held more truths than readers could handle.

— — — — — — — — — — —

Since the 2003 invasion of Iraq, an estimated 450,000 Iraqi civilians have died. And 4,491 American servicemen and women have died as well. I keep seeing these two numbers reported side by side, as if the numbers equal. They do not equal. Not by any calculus that can be qualified. Another number is how much the war has cost in terms of American dollars, as if that means anything against the other numbers.

— — — — — — — — — — —

We see more massacres in America than in any other country. That's a statement that needs cross-reference, of course, but since we are so amenable to stories being spun without adherence to any criteria, I'll let it stand.

We watch massacre after massacre, at home and abroad, and pull out our tired old clichés after each one. We mention bad guys and good guys. We deal only in absolutes. You're either for us or against us. We believe war is peace, and only by engaging in one can we hope to find the other. We obfuscate our words in doublespeak. The only way to stop wars is with more wars. We also downsize that sentiment to the singularity of guns, which we are told constantly that if we outlaw, only outlaws will have them and that only good guys with them can stop bad guys with them, phrases not only that neatly divide the world into for or against, good or bad, never taking into consideration that there are degrees of control, but about which the facts tell us otherwise, even if we have taken leave of our common sense.

The difference is that peace is not the same as war. We all know that more of anything can never equal less of anything. These are stories: King Midas learns asceticism from his cursed touch; the true mother offers the lying mother her child rather than see it cut in half; Jesus feeds the multitudes with loaves and fishes. Of these three stories, one is a fable from which we are to learn, another a parable which we should ponder to find meaning. The last is a miracle only God could give.

— — — — — — — — — — —

There are, of course, other atrocities. I've only listed a few here. The story of the massacre at No Gun Ri struck me because I had never heard of it. It happened twenty-two years before I was born, and though I consider myself an educated man, drawn to history and wars and stories that incorporate both, I had never heard of the rail bridge or the shooting or how many military units were unprepared and untrained in the first few weeks of the war. Some men threw down their rifles. Others were just following orders. I didn't know how many people died or how the water ran red and how some men still hear the screams of the children.

These are the stories that cut and scar, that break the skin and shake the heart in its cage, that make us question what we have heard all our lives, but there are others that give some semblance of hope. Robert M. Carroll, then a twenty-five-year-old first lieutenant, was not convinced the refugees were enemies and ordered his men to cease firing. He then herded a young boy to safety and tried to comfort the women and children.

James T. Kerns fired over the refugees' heads, refusing to take aim.

Delos Flint wouldn't fire "at anybody in the tunnel like that. It was civilians just trying to hide," he said.

"You can't kill people just for being there," Col. Gilmon A. Huff told Associated Press reporters forty-nine years later, which makes me wonder how long he had been thinking about it.

—————————————

The emperor fiddles while Rome burns. The barbarians are at the gate. Lot's wife looks back and is turned to salt. Orpheus's wife looks back and is sucked down into Hades, but what if she runs ahead, brushing past the man who saved her? What if Odysseus hears the faint wisp of song and becomes enthralled, never returns to kill the suitors, lives a long and full life carving little animals from driftwood washed up on the island? Has a hundred children who grow up and leave home but always pine in their hearts for the songs of their mothers? Penelope marries all the suitors and has a hundred children of her own and is happier with her grief unburdened? Lot's wife never becomes a condiment? The barbarians bang on the gate but only ask for water before riding on, and the emperor's songs quench the fire consuming the empire as a new era of peace and prosperity begins?

Say the dragon never steals the treasure. The wolves never stray from the forest, and the little girl never strays inside. Say the princess is never caged in the consulate. The knight-errant never lowers the visor that obscures his vision. Say we check the closet before sleeping and sweep the flashlight under the bed. We allow the pied piper to lead us into foreign lands where we learn from the past.

Say we can change the stories we tell and the way we tell them.

Not long after my grandfather died, my mother sent me a letter he had written while he was stationed in Korea during the war. I had just moved to North Carolina to attend graduate school, to try to learn to write, to make sense of the stories we tell ourselves, and she wanted me to have the letter.

My grandfather had spent the end of World War II driving generals through the ruins of European cities. Before I moved, he told me of the hollowed-out remnants of Dresden, the fallen walls of Berlin. Of how the Allied forces commandeered anything they wanted from the German civilians like dragons stealing treasure.

In Korea he worked in a hospital in Pusan. In the letter, he mentioned the poor conditions. The houses were mud and people slept on the floors and the fields were fertilized with human waste. My grandfather wrote of all these things to shed light on how the people lived in the part of the world he found himself in, and I find myself wondering about a man who sees war but worries about the conditions of the civilians. He said there were no plows except crooked sticks, and one wonders if they were all beaten into swords. He mentioned the hard labor of the villagers, that planting and harvesting and threshing were all done by hand, and it strikes me now to wonder why he paid attention to such things and why he talked about only them.

Late in the letter he mentions a cease-fire, his hope of the war ending. He mentions my mother, an infant at the time. He says he'd give anything to see her again, and there is in this line the hidden heart of the writer, who would give anything to go home, to return to where he was before he saw all the things he saw.

Those sentiments are subtle, however, like the description of the squalid conditions, the listing of hardships that aren't his. I have to read what isn't there, the things he doesn't say. I don't know if he ever heard of No Gun Ri. If he felt the rumble of the earth beneath him as tanks treaded past, if he heard the quick loud cough of machine-gun fire. If he saw the men come back from the front missing limbs. If he zipped closed, there in the hospital, the black bags over sightless eyes.

I only know what he wrote in his letter. His hope of returning. Of a cease-fire. Of an end to all this.

And this story:

"The hunting over here is nothing short of wonderful," my grandfather wrote. "The rice paddies abound in ring-necked pheasants. A lake some 10 or 12 miles east of here is on the flyway for waterfowl. One day I estimate I saw 200 ducks and geese, but they were too far away to fire at. It was late in the evening and the ducks were on the other side of the lake. This lake is bounded on one side by almost insurmountable cliffs while a road runs parallel to the other shoreline. So, with uncanny instinct, the duck and geese fly next to the hills."

He goes on to say local fishermen could be hired to row out beneath the flyway, and while I imagine he did this, I also imagine he did not fire. That he stood in the little boat and watched the geese veering overhead, that he heard their cries echo off the cliffs and their song stayed his hand, that he just watched them mirrored on the lake as they winged south for winter, their shadows thrown across the cliff face in the last rays of the sun. That he wondered how the world could be full of such beauty and sadness at the same time, though I would tell him now that the geese did not shy away from man by instinct but by learned behavior.

— — — — — — — — — — —

When I first heard the story of No Gun Ri, I wondered why what happened at the rail bridge was covered up for fifty years. Or if it were only one story of so many that it got lost in the rumors of war. I wondered what stories would come from the Gulf besides the waving of flags, how many bodies would be buried in bunkers or uncovered once the rubble was cleared. I wondered if other stories in our country are covered up because we cannot look at the unsavory past or because we want to believe a different story, one in which we only wage war to bring peace and which only bombs and bullets can pacify. That blessed are the mighty and the mighty never falter. That the dragon deserves the treasure. That the princess wants to be caged. That it's okay to throw others to the wolves if it will save ourselves.

When the Russian brothers turned back from tossing the bride and groom, they had reached the walls of the village. The villagers had heard the cries in the night and turned out of their homes to help. Holding torches and pitchforks to fight the wolves, they witnessed what occurred.

The two brothers were banished. They made their way to America, in hope of a new start, with the chance to leave the past behind.

— — — — — — — — — — —

Didion concluded that writing never helped her understand the narrative of her life, but I say stories are the only thing that can help us make sense. She claims events are random, that we attempt to force story upon these random events, and perhaps I do so here in an attempt to shape order from disparate threads, to hope that the stories we hear have some meaning.

What I question are the narratives we cling to, from our might to our right to our invoking of God's name in an attempt to ameliorate the casualties we inflict upon ourselves, to bless the casualties we inflict upon others.

The world, Anne Frank wrote, is gradually being turned into a wilderness. The approaching thunder will destroy us. The falcon cannot hear the falconer. The last unicorn has been slain in the last reach of forest. The hounds have been released and are running over the salted fields. The fox is in the henhouse, the crows are in the corn. The inmates have taken over the prison; they have taken over the asylum.

Despite all that, a fourteen-year-old girl taught us that it could all come right. "In spite of everything, I still believe," she wrote. There is more to that sentence but I will end it there—I still believe. That there's a narrative to our lives we can learn from and that we can form the narrative to find meaning. That though we live in a world of fiction, stories offer us salvation if we can find the strength to tell them true.

SHOCK AND AWE

Late one night as a child, in bed in my room, with heat lightning quaking sourceless on the horizon and lighting the world in quick flashes, I convinced myself the missiles had flown and the bombs had begun to fall. After each flash came a low concussion like the coughs of my cancer-killed uncle, and while waiting for the brief white light that came before forever and forever, I fell to my knees and asked God to spare this sinful world. Down the road a quarter mile, I could see in the lightning strikes the spire of the Baptist church where I'd first learned of the lake of eternal fire and heard grown men speak of the end as a thing soon to be, and kneeling there on the floor of my unclean room I swore it had come.

This was 1983, not long after the Soviet Union's early warning system erroneously reported the launch of American Minuteman missiles, and the world came as close as it had ever come to nuclear war. I was eleven years old, voice not yet deepened, the Cold War still as cold as the nuclear winter scientists theorized would descend on us after the bombs fell and the world caught fire and the smoke from the burning obscured the sun. The Four Horsemen would come riding down from the sky in missile streaks, and those distant flashes of lightning would grow to envelop us all. In my elementary school we had learned what to do in case of nuclear war, sirens went off at regular intervals, and on spring afternoons when black clouds boiled out of the west and bent the trees horizontal, we crawled under our desks as the wind howled and howled and our born-again teacher led us in prayer or read to us the story of Jesus calming the storm.

This was it, I was sure. I'd never seen lightning like this, every few seconds the world gone white and bright as day. The tops of the trees stirred in a wind that didn't touch the ground, as if unseen airplanes streaked low overhead, and long growls of thunder joined one with another until the ground shook and the windows rattled violently in their panes. I've never been as scared as I was at that moment, with the only exceptions being the two times my wife lay giving birth and I wore a pacing hole at the foot of the hospital bed and made myself sick with worry until heads crowned and these tiny beautiful daughters came crying into the world. Any second now, I thought that night, thin wires of fire would fall out of the heavens and everything we knew and loved would end. Only a few weeks before, the Soviet Union had shot down a Korean airliner with a U.S. congressman on board, and every storm that raged through our town seemed another sign that the end was near. The pastors preached it from the pulpits, and even the president seemed to fear what might fall on us out of the sky.

Twenty years later, in March 2003, as airplanes began to descend toward Baghdad, a spring storm sent the shadows of the trees swaying on the walls of my daughters' bedroom, and they woke crying after a sudden clap of thunder sounded loud as the last days of the earth. My wife and I rushed to hold them, whisper soft words in their ears. Our daughters were six and three then, terrified of the violent world outside the window, and so we stood there giving them what words we could to comfort them, saying, "It will be all right" and "Everything's fine."

Later we'd hear the news that another Gulf War had begun, not far from the Plains of Megiddo, where prophecy says the final battle will take place. We'd see the footage of what looked like lightning over a dark city, hear the harsh thundering cough of too-close bombs, the dull drum of machine-gun fire, the cameras capturing the night all shaking, the sky rattling in each explosion. Smoke rose like mist from the river, and children woke to sounds they did not understand, as brief white light flashed on the quaking bedroom walls.

MY NEW
WAR ESSAY

Will have the words shit and fuck everywhere. Also Jesus Christ and goddammit to hell and Please God No. Shit and fuck will be used when describing the action of war, the bullets and bombs. The others when describing the aftermath of the first.

My new war essay will be amorphous, random forms in morning fog. It will show shadows in sunlight, the moon ringed with frost on a cold night while bombs bloom skyward, phantom shapes shimmering the stars. There will be cumulus clouds over the heartland, snowcapped mountains, rivers running to oceans.

Early in the essay there will be clubs, hurled rocks, then swords and spears. There will be walls and moats and then castles, gunpowder, cannons, flintlocks, repeating rifles. The industry of war will continue to grow, until there are all kinds of bombs, landmines, missiles that lock on to targets the sizes of small children, and men who stand around harrumphing and crowing and pleased, believing they have achieved something good with every new discovery, every invention of war.

There will be nothing good in my new war essay. There will be no birdsong before first light, no blue afternoons so beautiful it hurts to look at them. No stars flung across a night sky. There is no time for that. There will only be cold mud and dry dust. Freezing rain and snow high in the mountains, 1,000-degree heat in the depths of the desert. Just thunder and lightning, earthquakes, hurricanes, smog. Some of it will be real. The rest only imagined or caused.

— — — — — — — — — — —

Fuck. Shit. Goddammit to hell.

— — — — — — — — — — —

There will be TV screens in my new war essay, lots of TV screens. Some of them will show soldiers in the streets of foreign cities, bullets ricocheting off buildings in little splinters of concrete. Others will show grainy night-vision litanies of antiaircraft streaking skyward and the great green glowing of bombs mushrooming in the distance. Still others will have troops returning while people wave flags, and still others—though they will be hard to find—will show bodies bloated in the streets.

My new war essay will be covered with blood, and halfway through, some kid will come home missing a leg and everyone will pretend it is still there until finally an old friend—the closest friend, the one who will later get drunk and press the heels of his hands hard against his cheekbones—will make a joke about Hopalong Cassidy and everyone will laugh a little uneasily.

In my new war essay there will be lots of rape. Plenty of pain. More murder and mayhem than stars in the exploded sky. There will be cracks and splinters, rocks and sand. Ricochets and high-pitched whining, the dull drone of engines, the thud of bombs off in the distance. There will be lots of bombs, lots of bullets, lots of flies, for it seems there are always flies in any war essay, and my new one will be no different—flies then, crawling on unseeing eyelids that shine like dull glass. Flies humming and buzzing like the paired planes overhead or the electric wires hissing in the street.

——— ——— ——— ——— ——— ——— ——— ——— ——— ——— ———

There will be white space in my new war essay. For reflection. A brief respite from the bombs and bullets careening around inside our skulls.

——— ——— ——— ——— ——— ——— ——— ——— ——— ———

But not much. Because with too much reflection, the idea of war makes no sense. And my new war essay—any war essay—has to make sense.

There will be no marches in my new war essay, no drums, no songs being sung, unless they are forlorn cadences about soldiers lying dead in the rain or bands on flag-filled streets echoing off the buildings, martial music striking up from speakers mounted on a military jeep. Any speeches will be kept short. They will confirm the need of what we are doing. They will provoke our patriotism and prove that providence has guided us here.

My new war essay will not slink through the streets like a dog. It will come brightly painted with slogans, and men in gray suits will cheer my new war essay from pulpits while people below them believe the words they spin into existence. There will be lots of flags. All colors, all sizes, all countries, little stick flags waving or jewelry flags pinned to lapels or bullet-riddled flags hanging limply from rusted poles above walls where twisting wires and broken shards of glass keep out the uninvited. People will salute the flags and bow to them because at the heart of war are flags, symbols of separation between us and them.

My new war essay will be set somewhere far away. (I don't want a new war essay where we live, do you?) So it will be set in Afghanistan or Iraq or Sierra Leone or along the Mexican-American border where carrion birds sit on telephone poles, waiting, while the dead lie in the streets and the occasional outburst of automatic weapons echoes and whines.

Shit. Fuck. Goddammit to hell.

There will be no human interest stories in my new war essay because war has no interest in humans. There will be dreams, but all of them will end with lightning or fire, some physical manifestation of what we already know.

My new war essay will use the words "freedom" and "democracy" and "liberation" and the phrases "maintaining order" and "stabilizing the region" and "pacification." It will be named "Operation New War Essay," and that name will capture the hearts and minds of the people on our side while showing us what we have to do to the people on the other side. It is a name chosen for its ability to strengthen our resolve and steel our softened hearts for the job that lies ahead.

It will be contradictory. We will fight for peace. We will kill to save lives. We will destroy so that we can rebuild. It will proclaim to be an essay about peace. It will go so far as to proclaim that all war is about peace, and in my new war essay there will be many who believe that.

Of course there will be hatred and misunderstanding. There will be fistfights and more curses—shit! fuck! goddamn!—and screaming and things being thrown. There will be people shaking their fists in anger and banging tabletops, their eyes as hard and wild as the sentences they speak. We'll all be able to find, in my new war essay, reasons to blow up people based on ethnicity, race, religious belief, sexual orientation, hair color or eye color or skin color, which hand they favor, if they like chocolate or strawberry ice cream more, the Steelers or the Cowboys, sweet potatoes or regular potatoes or no potatoes at all, and of course, you, the reader, will know that I am having a bit of fun at your expense, but you will also realize that many of the examples I come up with are just as silly as any of the other hundreds of thousands of reasons we have gone to war in the past.

There will be missing limbs in my new war essay. And missing children. Missing husbands, wives, brothers, sisters, mothers, fathers. There will be missing teeth and missing holes in people's lives, long stretches of time where they only worried about surviving or worried whether the characters in my new war essay would ever come home. Buildings will miss windows and walls. Cities will miss running water, and the children who miss food in the areas of my new war essay where food is missing will run through streets missing buildings with their stomachs distended and flies swirling around them and carrion birds waiting. My new war essay will be repetitive. It will show the same images over and over, mostly death, places where even life is now missing, great swaths of land missing what once lived there, before my new war essay was written.

— — — — — — — — — — — —

My new war essay will not make people feel bad though. Because it is only an essay. The images may be real, but once we finish reading we can put it down. We can walk away and forget about the bullets and bombs and missing limbs and missing lives, and even if we do become overwhelmed by the words that are not written in my new war essay—the words that can never be written about war because there really are no words that can ever capture what war is—we will be bolstered by my new war essay because more and more and more, my new war essay will come to assert, again and again, that it is right and is always right and has always been right. It has to, to believe in itself. It has to deny any logic—it has to drown out any opposition. For there will come a time when someone will question my new war essay, and then the smoke lying heavy in the streets will become not so much a screen as a silhouette. And then there will come a dull silence hovering over everything, all quiet but for a rusty wailing in the distance. And then the war will begin.

WHAT HAPPENS NEXT

FORT CHAFFEE, ARKANSAS: 1983

In the long afternoons the distant bombs sounded like thunder. The windows of our classrooms rattled as fighters from Chaffee a few miles away streaked the slanted sky. Helicopters hovered like funnel clouds, and often we could not tell what was causing the thunder, so when the sirens erupted we huddled in the hallways or beneath our desks, and I could not say now whether we hid from the weather or weapons.

When school let us out for summer, we swam in the senseless heat, craning our necks to count the vapor trails of fighters overhead. Smoke rose from rents in the hills where bombs ignited the dry brush. In the cool stream, we sunk to our eyelids, submersed as if water would save us, but back on dry land we could feel the rumble of the earth through the floors of our small shoes.

When my father drove through the base, the roads were patched, and it took me years to realize that here was where the fire we felt on August afternoons fell from the sky. The dark spots on the asphalt were where holes had been filled in from errant bombs. Steel fences switched along beside us, topped by coils of wire like twists of fear. My father stopped when a convoy crossed the road, the mirror-eyed heads of the soldiers swiveling as they passed. In the distance the rusting hulks of bombed trucks rattled in the wind, and on the hills and ridges where the vapor trails ended, the splintered trunks of old-growth oak scratched at the sky.

On the main base the barracks hunched over the torn earth like squatters in rows or the way we've tried to order our lives, to make sense of things too vast to piece together. Paint peeled back from the boards like dead skin, and the windows didn't look like soulless, staring eyes so much as eyes bereft of sight.

This is where it began for me; this is what I remember: phantom fighters screaming overhead and the earth trembling below, as fire fell from the sky. Until the trembling is always there. The fighters are always on approach and the bombs are always about to fall. There are always men with mirrored eyes, with booted feet.

FORT SILL, OKLAHOMA, BASIC TRAINING: 1990

At the end of each day, we counted down, marked it off the calendar because we had survived, an occasion we deemed worthy of celebration because said survival was not always assured. But as lights-out approached, after we had made it through the tear gas chamber and did not get shot on the rifle range, after we had performed more push-ups than our muscles could possibly manage and still did not die, we celebrated.

We did not know then that we weren't supposed to die. It seemed that the drill sergeants meant to kill us, surrounded as we were by bombs and bullets, by fires and fighters overhead, by long days in summer heat. But this was only training, our bodies beaten down to be built back up, our psyches attacked to make us tougher, so we struggled through, celebrating the close of each day, when we could shut our eyes for a few hours.

When we woke in the morning, the fear returned to fill our insides. Calls and cadences were already erupting around us, men scrambling madly as if war had come. Fort Sill was live-fire, like Chaffee, which I had grown up around, and bombs were bursting in air all over the base even before first light, the earth still shaking as if in memory of all the missiles that had flown before. When we ran in the darkness before dawn, explosions erupted like lightning, and when the sun came up, the air stood hazed in the heat.

All day, fires broke out on the empty ranges. We aimed our rifles and set off claymore mines, starting more fires. We swam blind through the tear gas chamber and learned how to administer antidotes in case of biological war, a phrase that carries the word "logical" inside it but cannot possibly be.

In the afternoons, we lay prone among the insects. In some field or scratch of forest we radioed enemy movements, playing at war like men with much thicker skin. When night fell over the forest, the trip wires went up and tracer fire streaked skyward. In the distance, the bombs were still falling.

We did not know that a new war would soon start. That the bombs would begin falling and would not stop. We were not yet given to the introspection that would come later, only the hope that we might survive to sleep and wake another day.

So when the day ended, we gathered around Ebel's bunk, shirtless as the days we were born. Sykes drumrolled on the wall of a metal locker. Richardson hummed reveille. Ebel, with a Sharpie his mother had sent, marked off the day with a big X and we all cheered, one day closer to graduation, when we could leave behind the bombs and the bullets, the place where surviving each day was something to be celebrated.

ARKANSAS TECH UNIVERSITY, THE NIGHT THE WAR BEGAN: 1991

We drove twenty miles on sheets of ice to the nearest liquor store. Winter here, and cold, the interstate empty but for a few fools like us and a dozen cars abandoned along the shoulder, windshields blanked by ice.

On the way back we slipped through side streets—smashing mailboxes, spinning wheels, engine shrieking into the silent night. Liquored up already, we celebrated canceled classes, knowing that tomorrow the halls of learning would stand vacant and our heads hungover while we slept into the afternoon.

So as the snow started to fall in the cold night, we hurled empty bottles into yards, plowed over trash cans as the snow piled higher, left a laughing swath of destruction in the still air behind us, as if we had been drawn to destroy, perhaps because of the spirits running through our veins or only our own spirits, our constant climb toward obliteration.

Halfway home we lost control of the car on the ice and slid sideways toward a bridge abutment. We whipped the wheel around and the back end spun out and suddenly we were leaning toward the end of our lives. We slid on toward the bridge and our last breaths, before finally righting ourselves, the tires catching and the crash averted. We pulled to the side of the road and sat quiet while the windshield fogged like smoke from bombs blooming in the cold cab. The roads were empty. There were no cars anywhere else in the world, as if everything had disappeared and the rest was indeed silence.

After a time, we put the car in drive and crept carefully the rest of the way, taking silent pulls from the bottle and thinking how we had cheated death. Almost home, and safe, we slid into a ditch and rocked there as the engine died, forced now to walk through the night. We stopped occasionally to pass the bottle or piss in someone's yard, our shadows shimmering in the streetlights and the whiskey working inside us, warm lights glowing through the windows of the apartments all around, nothing falling from the sky but snow. When we get home, we will watch the start of the first Gulf War, the fires rising over the city of Baghdad in the green light of night vision, and we will cheer so loudly the neighbors will wake to bang on the wall, but we will be too busy celebrating to care about anyone else.

NORTH CAROLINA AND IRAQ, THE NIGHT THE WAR BEGAN: 2003

A student of mine is called from a class that is not about sucking chest wounds to one that is. From history to history. From theater to theater.

That night, I watch again the fires unfurling over Baghdad. A new kind of war, we are told, though the same sounds are still used, the same old images we've seen on our screens: the blaze of sudden bombs, the brief white light that might mean forever for some folks. The screams and sirens, the antiaircraft fire streaking skyward, same as we all saw twelve years before. Second verse, same as the first, though I am sober this time and it will go on much longer as well. As if we have learned no lessons except how to treat the wounds that always arise.

GREENSBORO, NORTH CAROLINA, WATCHING THE MILITARY CHANNEL WITH THE SOUND OFF: 2012

Which I do, late at night sometimes when my children are asleep and I don't want them to wake to the sounds of bombs or bullets, when I wish them to sleep in peace a few hours more.

On the screen, the images roll past—missiles streaking in strands of smoke, planes in convoy overhead, men marching in ragged rows—but the cannons don't cough. Artillery doesn't shatter the silent night. The airplanes don't drone nor do the shovels spark when striking rocks in foxholes or shallow graves. The carcasses don't exhale or empty themselves of everything they ever ate. The wind slips through the frozen trees, but on the screen there is only silence.

The tanks don't tread nor do the turrets twist. The bombs only bloom silently skyward, our eyes wondering how there can be that much of anything in all the world: fire, fear, fatalities. The trumpets don't sound for victory or retreat, because the war is always on, blinking black and white off the walls. The crowds don't cheer nor does martial music mount up from a military jeep whose shadow is thrown on the rubble of ruined cities as it races for the front, carrying codes you couldn't understand with all the explanation in the universe.

The radios don't squawk or sputter or spew static in sharp, quick spikes like machine-gun bursts or missile strikes. You can't hear the cries or the commands. You'll never hear the sirens. So when you finally fall asleep and accidentally elbow the remote and the sound comes screaming in, you'll only scramble to find the button that brings back the silence. You're still not listening. No matter how many times you've seen the show.

TOO MANY NIGHTS NOW

I wake from a dream in which I am back at military training, among the classrooms and the clash of claymores, the hot wake of wind from the report of rifles. Booted feet echo through the hallways, and forced voices call cadence while the light bends in the shock wave of bombs.

Or I am sitting in the chow hall, where we chewed with our mouths open like boys in men's skin, peeling fresh fruit while Wilkins tells us of women he wants and Buist keeps saying "boob." Or we are lining up for first aid or we are filing out to the field. We are climbing on buses. We are playing with our balls. Someone says "fuck" like a curse or call to arms.

In my sleep, I see the faces of the men who stood beside me, hoarse from answering every question in a too-tough voice, cheeks still smooth as if in elementary school, before the shaving and the shouting and the shoving one another when the days grew too long. We might still be boys pretending to be men for all we have learned, the way we were once upon a time, our young minds not understanding why our scared voices sound so old. Somewhere, a newsreel is announcing another war or another school shooting or another terrorist attack. We are climbing into bathrooms to hide from the bullets. We are playing with our balls. Someone says boob or fuck or bomb or fear.

I walk the rifle range and the obstacle course, which makes me think of recess and races, start and finish lines toed in mud, and this is when the dream changes, and instead of in the military I am now back in second grade. I hear booted feet coming down the concrete hallways, and I am not sure whether they belong to men in masks or are the new shoes our mother bought before school started. I know this dream returns because anytime I hear of another war starting or a school shooting, I feel like a child back in a classroom looking out at a world I don't understand. In my middle age I dream often of what I might have done to make our planet a safer place, whether in the barracks of an army base or outside my second-grade classroom, but what I come back to most often is that, despite a lifetime of looking back, I am unprepared for what will happen next.

WHEN THE WAR BEGAN

The war in Afghanistan is older than my dog, my cat, my car, my favorite pair of jeans, the Japanese maple in my front yard, the grocery store I frequent, my credit card, some translations of the Bible, the last three books of the Harry Potter series, the iPod, most cell phones, WikiLeaks, YouTube, Facebook, Twitter, the Jonas Brothers' career, and the obsession we have with the coming zombie apocalypse. It is older than the finger paintings I have on the wall of my study, older than all the skin cells on your body, older than all the hummingbirds and human eyelashes in the world.

I have lived in my current house for fewer years than the war has gone on. I have only lived in one house for longer. Neither of my daughters has ever lived in the same house for as long as the war has gone on. Neither of them owns anything as old as the war, not stuffed animals or real animals or friendships, with the exception of torn copies of *Goodnight Moon* and *Where the Wild Things Are* that were once mine, books I have read to my children so many times since the war began I have lost count.

The war in Afghanistan is almost as old as my younger daughter. She was born fourteen months before the September II attacks. She was too young to know what had happened or what it might mean. I remember where I was and what I was doing that day, but so does everyone else.

— — — — — — — — — — —

The war in Afghanistan has lasted longer than World War I, World War II, and the Korean War. It has lasted longer than the Civil War and the Revolutionary War and the War of 1812. It has lasted longer than three of the four great Crusades, the first Gulf War, the Six-Day War, the Yom Kippur War, the Falklands War, the Spanish-American War, the Mexican-American War, the Barbary Wars, the invasions of Panama, Grenada, Somalia, the Dominican Republic, Lebanon, and the conflicts in Bosnia and Libya and Kosovo.

The Vietnam War lasted 103 months, from the Gulf of Tonkin Resolution to the last withdrawal of American troops. The war in Afghanistan has lasted 120 months so far. An active couple could have eleven or twelve children in that time. The oldest of those children would have learned to walk and talk, ride a bicycle, skip stones, splash through muddy creeks, rub food into her hair, smile, laugh, sing, dance, cry. She would have entered elementary school and learned to finger-paint, drink chocolate milk from little cartons, read, play hopscotch, jump rope, and many other games such as cops and robbers and cowboys and Indians and war.

When we played war, my brother and I burned our little green army men. We'd use matches or lighters or gasoline and watch them melt into pools of plastic, but in less time than the war has gone on we grew out of that.

— — — — — — — — — — —

Roughly 30 to 40 percent of marriages last less time than the war in Afghanistan. Some divorces turn into little wars of their own, full of shouting and accusations and dishes thrown against the wall. I've even heard that children who have gone through a divorce are more likely to become divorced, although it's possible I am conflating that saying with the one about children who were beaten being more likely to beat their own children.

If the war in Afghanistan were married, I suspect it would be to the war in Iraq. They have lots in common: dry, barren, war-torn lands, a hidden enemy, a confused and frightened population, a tenuous idea on both sides of how the war might end. They both have bombs going off in the distance and sand blown into everything by the constant wind and buildings destroyed by years of war, and when we see pictures or videos of either country we often see children playing in the streets while their parents worry what might happen to them.

The war in Afghanistan just celebrated its tenth anniversary. Traditionally, this is the tin anniversary. The first metallic alloy was bronze, made of tin and copper. It ushered in a new age of weaponry and warfare.

— — — — — — — — — — —

When my grandfather was alive, he used to tell me all the things they didn't have when he was growing up: computers, air conditioning, Velcro, television, telephones, credit cards, bar codes, the pill, VCRs, ATMs, word processors, video games, microwaves, automatic windows, car alarms, jet fighters, and nuclear weapons. He was born in November of 1916, two years before the armistice was signed and World War I ended. He was married on December 6, 1941, a day before World War II began.

He has been dead now for fifteen years, less time than the war in Afghanistan, and I imagine conversations we might have if he were still alive. When I joined the military, he began to tell me stories about his own service, although his stories never mentioned war directly. Rather he told me of the rice paddies in Korea or driving through the French countryside in World War II.

No bombs or bullets, no artillery or airplanes, no body bags or corpses staring unseeing at the sun.

He once told me there were many things now—like automatic transmissions and refrigerators—that he would not wish to live without. War was not one of them.

— — — — — — — — — — —

On a larger scale, ten years is not a long time. Saturn's ponderous orbit of the sun takes almost thirty years, and Halley's Comet comes once every seventy-five. The Hundred Years' War lasted 116 years. Cortes destroyed Tenochtitlan 500 years ago. The Bronze Age lasted 2,000 years. For close to 160 million years, dinosaurs thumped around the earth, roaring and hunting and scavenging and killing and dying before some greater cataclysm roared out of the sky. Before that, the earth was a hot rock sizzling through space, and before that, most scientists believe, our universe was born in a flash of violence.

— — — — — — — — — —

Since the war began, I have quit smoking and started again, quit, started, and quit. My older daughter has grown two feet, four inches. My younger daughter has grown over three feet. They have both started and finished elementary school. They have lost over thirty baby teeth. I have finished graduate school, taught for close to a decade, seen my students become teachers and lawyers and doctors who plan on making a difference in the world. I have watched the leaves turn colors and fall from the trees and go rattling down the sidewalk in the winter eleven times. Mercury has spun around the sun forty-two times, and the moon has spun around the earth close to 300, changing as it goes from light to dark and back again.

Over a half dozen other conflicts have sprung up since the war in Afghanistan began, including the Arab Spring revolts, the new and most current Palestinian-Israeli conflict, and an increase in violence in the drug war along the Mexican-American border. There are currently over a dozen conflicts, wars, or insurgencies escalating, dying down, or simmering, in four of the seven continents.

— — — — — — — — — — —

The United States has built military bases in seven countries since the war in Afghanistan began. I lived for many years within thirty miles of a live-fire base. On bombing days, we could feel the ground rumble beneath our feet. The dishes in our cabinets rattled and shook, the wind chimes rippled without wind.

Fighter jets streaked past in the fall, their noise trailing behind them. At night they flashed radiant signals that flickered overhead. The land lay scorched all winter, until spring returned and new grass broke through the crusted earth. Then the bombs came again, and the fires, the horizon distant with smoke haze and the smell of scorched earth inside us.

Most of the time we ignored what was going on around us. We did not wake in the night to the sound of fighters screaming overhead or bombs falling in the distance. Other times, it seemed the ground was always shaking, and there was nothing you could do to stop it.

— — — — — — — — — — —

The are no reliable figures for the number of lives lost in Afghanistan. There are no reliable numbers for civilian casualties, active landmines, houses blown up, children with missing limbs, wives without husbands, or soccer balls deflated by bullet holes. There are no reliable numbers for the deaths that have occurred from starvation, disease, exposure, lack of medical treatment, or the fear of what might come out of the sky.

There are no figures for children who listen to the rumbling of bombs in the distance or fighters streaking overhead. There is nothing that mentions the flat cough a landmine must make when it tears off a child's leg or the way bullets ricochet off buildings or the whine and echo they make in the mountains as they careen among the rocks. There are no statistics for the number of buildings that have crumbled under the weight of bombs or the number of people who have dug through the rubble, listening to screams muffled by stone and dust until they fade away like the distant sounds of airplanes.

There are figures relating the number of suicides by soldiers returned from war. And the number of soldiers who came back missing an eye or an arm. And the number suffering from post-traumatic stress disorder, although the numbers don't tell how many of them sit alone in a tiny room drinking vodka all day and watching people out the window or the number who can't sleep at night or the number who feel the ground shaking beneath them all the time. Some psychologists believe those suffering from post-traumatic stress disorder are still fighting the war, years after it has ended.

There are no reliable figures for the amount of money the war has cost, but if war were a business, the war in Afghanistan would need a government bailout.

——— ——— ——— ——— ——— ——— ——— ——— ——— ——— ———

There has been war almost continuously in Afghanistan since 1978. That's over thirty years. That's Mercury around the sun 125 times. That's Max sailing to the land of the Wild Things over 10,000 times, over 10,000 combs and brushes and bowls full of mush, 10,000 old ladies whispering hush. That's 3 Vietnam Wars or 6 Civil Wars or 1,825 Six-Day Wars.

Thirty years ago, I was in first grade. At recess we played football every day. We lined up opposite each other and tried to control the field, tried to take over what the other team held. Sometimes we got into fights, as children will.

Thirty years is older than both my children put together. It is half of my father's life. Thirty years ago, he was still in the National Guard. I woke some Saturday mornings to watch him shave and put on his uniform. When he bent to kiss me he smelled of aftershave and shoe polish. I asked him if he would ever have to go to war and he said, "Not if I'm lucky, son."

I am trying to decide which is older: war or prayer.

The war in Afghanistan is made of unwashed clothing. It is made of dust and wind, exposed Kevlar fibers, and rocks. It is made of MREs, trip wire, flashlights attached to the ends of rifles that go bobbing up narrow stairways in the middle of the night, unshaved beards, mornings without sleep, scraps of food, and whispered conversations. It is made of death, as all war is.

The war in Afghanistan looks like unbrushed teeth. It looks like gangrene and mold and cockroaches scurrying to find new places to hide when the light comes on. It looks like cancer or tuberculosis or emphysema. It looks like unkempt hair and red eyes, dismembered toes with yellow nails, frozen earth, oil rainbows on unmoving water. It looks like trees skeletal with winter, blue haze of woodsmoke and real smoke and car exhaust hovering over the cities, a strange sky at night.

The war in Afghanistan sounds like rocket bursts in the distance or long stretches of wind howling over mountain flanks. It sounds like words that don't mean anything. It sounds like loudspeakers in the streets, muffled shouting, the laughter of children just before they fall silent. It sounds like coughing, low-throated whispers, an incoming whistling, rocks fountaining upward, dogs slinking through trash-littered alleys, snow falling in the last reaches of forest.

It smells like unwashed bodies and fear. It feels like scabbed-over wounds. It tastes like dirt and ashes.

I had just started graduate school when the war began. It was October, a Sunday, and the leaves must have been falling from the trees. I don't remember what I did that day or where I was. But on a normal Sunday in graduate school, I would have been sitting at a bar drinking and talking too loudly with writer friends about our desire to change the world with the words we would write. Walking home, the night would have been almost cool. We did not know then that the bombs had begun to fall. I would wake the next morning with a headache from drinking too much, my stomach sour and a horrible taste in my mouth as I listened to the news from halfway around the world. But the night the war began, I must have looked past the city lights to the stars hurling themselves through the sky like holes shot into the night. My children were at home in bed, blankets tucked in neatly to keep them warm and safe, and I must have walked toward them along the dark streets, in and out of patches of light, my head thrown back, happy with my place in the world, watching nothing but leaves fall from the sky.

IN THE HEART OF
THE COUNTRY

——— —— —— —— —— —— —— —— —— —— —— ——

At a university in northern Iowa a girl asked me if I would ever
let my daughters join the military. I had been invited as an author for the university's common reading, an anthology of short
stories in which I had published a fictional account of a soldier
struggling after returning from Afghanistan. The soldier had
lost a leg and shortly after coming back loses the other. Then he
loses his hand and has it replaced with chainsaws for fingers,
and the university had loved it enough to fly me in for three
days. The night before, I had given a speech on absurdity, literature, and the American soldier, and now I was here to share
my wisdom on the subjects. I didn't have the heart to tell them
I didn't have any wisdom, that, like most of us, I was only trying
to understand the absurdity that causes us to keep repeating the
same course of action.

The girl sat in the second row. She had long brown hair she
kept hooking behind her ears, and this was the fourth question she had asked, all of which had sent me struggling for an
answer: *How do you feel about your time in the service? Do you
ever want to go back? What was your favorite part about being in
the army?*

I could have told her my favorite moments in the army were the times we talked about going home, which would have answered all three questions, but I had spoken to six groups so far, each with more than a hundred students. This was the smallest, and most of the seats were empty. The big hall vaulted overhead, and my voice echoed like we were underwater. After the lecture the night before, I'd drunk beer in a bar with a former combat marine who'd driven three hours to hear me talk about war, which was absurd in itself, that I had somehow become an expert. He wanted to know how to write about what he'd seen, and I didn't have an answer except to say he needed to tell the truth.

But I had spoken too much already, my head hurt from the beer at the bar, and I wondered what good the truth would do anyway, so I didn't tell the girl she was the same age as my older daughter. I didn't say that when I was a child, I woke some nights scared of the end of the world and that fear has now manifested itself into a fear the world will end before my daughters can save it, or at least see some of it.

So I said we'd have to wait until that moment came. And if it did, my daughters and I would educate ourselves on the pros and cons of military life. We'd try to understand what it meant to serve in this new world, what it meant to wield a weapon for words like "freedom" and "democracy." That we would look, together, at the long history of our country, the service of her soldiers, and all the places those soldiers have been sent in service to such hard-to-define terms. We'd look at the movements that shaped us, the beliefs we collectively hold that we are the good guys and anyone who opposes us is bad. I'd tell them about my time in the military and how my beliefs changed after I got out, that I was proud of my service but now I question the constant need for it, and I'd say that war seems to be the default state we live in, that there's only a brief pause now between battles, before the shooting starts again.

But what I really thought was that for a few days in high school, I wore my uniform to classes. My recruiter paid me as a promotion—he thought seeing the uniform would get more boys my age to join the military. I was around the same age then as the girl at the university in Iowa, in the deep heart of the country, the age my daughters are, just old enough to join but without any of the wisdom one gets from walking around in the world.

I also did not tell her that ever since, instead of dreaming I'm at school in my underwear, I dream I'm in my uniform, head shaved and dog tags rattling beneath my brown shirt. And some afternoons years ago, picking up my daughters from elementary school, I arrived so late everyone else was gone. The war in Afghanistan was only a few years old, Iraq still an infant, and it was easy to believe then—because of the dreams, because of the military days, because of Desert Storm and all the other wars we've seen—that they had all been sent overseas: men and women, girls and boys, teachers and cafeteria workers. The classrooms were empty, the chairs all put away, and my boots echoed like bullets as I walked the long halls where I was the only one left.

After my talk, the girl will tell me that her parents are career military. That she is joining the air force as soon as she graduates, and I can tell from her voice that she grew up on military bases where fighters droned overhead and the shuddering boom of bombs broke the afternoon stillness. That the sound of bullets is nothing new, the march of booted feet only a backdrop to what's coming. Still, she seems so small. She hooks her hair once again as she listens to my answer. And my voice seems to boom in the almost empty ballroom, as if everyone else has disappeared and we're all that's left, those who have served, and those who soon will.

ACKNOWLEDGMENTS

Most of the men and women I knew in the military have moved on out of my life. It's the normal order of things, but I keep calling them back in writing, which also seems normal. It seems normal as well to speculate on what might have happened if I had stayed. Or, put another way, what might happen if we, our country, continue on our course.

This book, then, is for all the men and women who have served before me: my father and stepfather and grandfather especially, men who taught me what it meant to wear a uniform. It's for all those I served alongside in Basic Training and beyond. And it's for those who continue to question what service means and why we are so often called to do it.

I would also like to thank the editors, readers, and general support givers who have donated their time and expertise: Lucas Church at UNC Press I am especially grateful to for approaching me about military writing; Tracy Crow for her careful reading and kind remarks; Mike Kubista for asking where the messed-up cadences were; the good folks at Northern Iowa University for bringing me to speak; and editors Donald Anderson, Robert Atwan, Jonathan Franzen, Dinty Moore, Ander Monson, John D'Agata, Okla Elliott, Jay Jennings, Jac Jemc, David Lazar, Grant Tracey, Vince Gotera, Richard Mathews, Keith Rebec, and Tom Dooley for publishing these essays.